Bicycling

COMPLETE BOOK OF
ROAD CYCLING SKILLS

REVISED AND UPDATED 2nd EDITION

Also by Jason Sumner:

75 Classic Rides Colorado

Bicycling 1,100 Best All-Time Tips

Bicycling
COMPLETE BOOK OF
ROAD CYCLING SKILLS

REVISED AND UPDATED 2nd EDITION

YOUR GUIDE TO RIDING FASTER, STRONGER, LONGER, AND SAFER

JASON SUMNER

RODALE.

RODALE
wellness

Live happy. Be healthy. Get inspired.

Sign up today to get exclusive access to our authors, exclusive
bonuses, and the most authoritative, useful, and cutting-edge
information on health, wellness, fitness, and living your life to
the fullest.

Visit us online at RodaleWellness.com
Join us at RodaleWellness.com/Join

Rodale books may be purchased for business or promotional use or for special sales.
For information, please write to: Special Markets Department, Rodale, Inc.,
733 Third Avenue, New York, NY 10017

Printed in the United States of America

Rodale Inc. makes every effort to use acid-free ⊗, recycled paper ♻.

Book design by Christina Gaugler

Photography by Jamie Squire/Getty Images (page 170); Mike Tittel (page 147); Gallery Stock (pages 11,
38, 80, 125); and all other photography by Matt Rainey/Rodale Images

Illustration by Joe Karapelou (page 183)

Library of Congress Cataloging-in-Publication Data is on file with the publisher.

ISBN: 978–1–62336–495–3   paperback

2   4   6   8   10   9   7   5   3   1   paperback

Distributed to the trade by Macmillan

🌱 RODALE.

Follow us @RodaleBooks on

We inspire health, healing, happiness, and love in the world.
Starting with you.

CONTENTS

PART FOUR: ESSENTIAL BICYCLE MAINTENANCE

PART FIVE: TRAINING ON AND OFF THE BIKE

PART SIX: FUELING YOUR RIDE

PART SEVEN: SKILL BUILDING 201

PART EIGHT: RACING AND RIDING FAST

INTRODUCTION

HOW TO USE THIS BOOK

In my humble opinion, there are three kinds of people in this world: those who love cycling, those who will love cycling, and those who will never try cycling. Point being, if you spend any time on a bike, you'll quickly discover its virtues as humankind's best invention. What else on this earth combines efficient transportation with life-enhancing exercise, joyful and exhilarating fun, and environmental friendliness all in one perfect package? Certainly nothing I can think of.

Cycling is also a true lifetime endeavor. You no doubt remember the sheer glee the first time you got rolling on your own without training wheels. And with any luck you'll all be riding bikes well into your golden years, that same wide smile across your face. Indeed, studies have shown that cycling improves concentration and memory function, reduces stress, and generally makes you happier and healthier.

But there is much more to riding a bike than what you learned as a kid. Basic skills such as steering, cornering, descending, braking, shifting gears, and even drinking from a water bottle all take practice. Indeed, the more you ride, the better (and faster) cyclist you'll become. Of course, a few pointers along the way come in handy, too.

That's where this book comes in. Within the following pages you'll find explanations detailing such things as how to buy a bike, tips for on-bike fueling, and how to train for your first century ride. There are also pointers on climbing, sprinting, and the all-important art of countersteering. The mental game is covered, too, with advice on how to overcome fear and use the power of positive thinking.

How best to use this book depends a lot on your current status as a cyclist. If you've already been riding for a few years, then it's likely you're looking for specific pointers. If so, then peruse the table of contents and/ or index to search for topics that address your current questions. Maybe you're trying to decide if you should get a coach (sidebar in Chapter 20). Or perhaps you want to better understand the nuances of riding in a rotating paceline (Chapter 36).

If you are brand new to this wonderful and amazing sport, start at the beginning of this book and work your way through. The sections and chapters follow a logical order that start with the basics, and then dive into more technical topics. Learn how to dial in your on-bike position (Chapter 2), how to dress (Chapter 4), and how best to use your brakes in a variety of situations (Chapter 7). If you run into a word or phrase you don't know, flip to the glossary in the back of this book.

But before you start flipping the pages, know this: If you are truly committed to becoming a better cyclist, then, like so many things in life, you would do well to set some goals. Whether you are riding for fun, fitness, weight loss, stress relief, or because you want to become the next Chris Froome, having goals will serve as motivation to ride, and ride better.

Finally, if you take nothing else away from this book, please memorize the following list and take its advice to heart, because it covers the 10 things that should be a part of every ride you do.

1. Check your bike: Properly inflate tires, lube chain as needed, and check brakes.

2. Wear a helmet: Always. No matter what. Period.

3. Carry basic tools: At a minimum always carry a spare tube, tire levers, an inflation device, and a small multitool.

4. Bring fuel: Your car needs gas. You need food and drink.

5. Be prepared: If there's even a remote chance of foul weather, make sure you have the right clothes.

6. Lather up: Skin cancer is not a joke. Wear sunscreen.

7. Bring ID: If something bad does happen, help the first responders by identifying yourself.

8. Pack your phone: Say what you will about smartphones, but they are great for calling for help or navigating when you get lost.

9. Be seen: Even just a basic blinky tail light will help drivers spot you. If you know you'll be out past dark, outfit your bike accordingly.

10. Have a plan: Know where you are going and how you are getting there.

Part One
GETTING STARTED

Chapter 1
BASICS OF BUYING A BIKE

Before you figure out the perfect on-bike position, before you devise the perfect training plan, and even before you head out for your first ride, you are going to need a bike. While many of the people who pick up this book already have their two-wheel situation sorted out, there are plenty who don't. Or maybe it's time for a new bike. Because, hey, who doesn't love a new bike?

So what is the best strategy for buying a bike? How can you assure the best bang for your buck without sacrificing on-road performance? Well, before you head to your local bike shop (or start perusing the Internet), you need to ask yourself some key questions.

Are your cycling goals modest? Are you simply seeking a comfortable companion that will allow you to spin easy miles and perhaps complete the local century ride? Or are you the more competitive type, with aspirations to race—and even win?

The answers to these questions will go a long way toward determining the type of bike you buy, be it one with a more relaxed "endurance" geometry (think more upright, like riding a Harley), or one that puts you in a low, aggressive position that allows you to cheat the wind at every turn. Either way, there will be dozens of potentially perfect bikes from which to choose.

Nearly all the major bike manufactures (and many of the smaller ones, too) offer an array of bikes to suit a variety of needs and desires. Take Specialized, for instance, which in 2016 had a road bike product line that included the Tarmac (lightweight race bike), Venge (aero race bike), Roubaix (endurance bike), and Diverge (gravel bike), plus specific offerings for track, cyclocross, and time trial. The same could be said of Trek, Giant, Scott, Cannondale, and so on.

Yes, it gets confusing quickly. And that's why doing research ahead of time is key. Read online product descriptions and product reviews. And, most important of all, know that there isn't one right answer. There are likely dozens of bikes capable of delivering the fun and performance you are looking for. In the end it might just come down to color. Because if you don't like the way your bike looks, what's the point?

Of course you also need to determine your budget. A top-shelf steed such as the Specialized S-Works Tarmac with Shimano Dura-Ace Di2 electronic shifting and lightweight carbon wheels will set you back nearly $10,000, while the basic Tarmac Sport is a more reasonable $2,000. And no matter what your budget, don't forget to account for the other necessary gear that you may need. Buying a helmet, cycling kit, and basic repair tools to fix a roadside flat can easily slice $200 to $300 from your budget. But all those items (especially the helmet) are every bit as necessary as the bike itself. If you don't carry the tools to fix a flat when you ride, then it's a matter of not if but when you will have to walk home or call your significant other for a ride.

Once you have at least a working idea about the type of bike and budget, it's time to find a local bike shop. I write this knowing full well that some bike buyers will opt to shop online. And that's fine, too. There are great deals to be had via the consumer-direct channel. Just make sure you have a full understanding of how your online seller will handle things such as warranties and returns. Personally, I prefer face-to-face transactions when it comes to cycling gear, which is why I recommend shopping local.

But don't just choose any shop. Find one you like, where the salespeople are friendly and willing to answer your questions without bias or attitude. Approach this as the beginning of a long, happy relationship, so don't go looking solely for the best deal.

Once you start the actual shopping process, remember first and foremost that it's important to find a bike that fits you. Manufacturers watch each other closely on price and components, especially on lower-priced models, so most of the significant differences between bikes lie in the fit and feel. Test ride at least a couple to find the bike that fits you best, and remember that a few minor adjustments can improve any bike. Like buying a custom suit, an extensive fit session will cost extra. But, the staff at a quality shop will help you with the essentials as a part of the sale. These services include setting the height and fore/aft position of the saddle on your new bike. Many shops will also help you evaluate whether your stem is the correct length, or if the handlebar is the right width and drop for your body type and needs. If you are unfamiliar with any of these cycling terms, please see the glossary located at the back of this book.

Pay closest attention to available size options and frame material. Major bike makers such as Trek, Specialized, and Giant typically offer each model in a number of frame sizes, which translates to a better fit. As for frame material, carbon fiber is the lightest, most expensive, and most common material on the market. If your budget is constrained, don't be afraid to check out a few aluminum models. It wasn't all that long ago that most top end bikes utilized alloy frames.

In addition to fit, look at a bike's components. Prioritize based on the value of key components, placing emphasis on wheels, the rear derailleur, and shifters in that order. If you're deliberating between two or more bikes (and have some extra time), look up the price for each bike's key individual components, then do a side-by-side cost analysis. You may find that one option is simply a better overall deal than another.

You'll also need to decide on preferred drivetrain style, choosing between a triple, double, or even a single ring crankset. Triples provide three chainrings, the smallest giving you easy gears for pedaling uphill, but add weight. Doubles feature two chainrings and work more smoothly, are lighter, and will give you most (but not all) of the same gears as compared with a triple. Single chainring setups serve a more specialized purpose such as criterium racing, time trialing, or off-road touring where simplicity of operation, weight savings, and ease of maintenance are key.

If your budget is around $3,000 or above, an electronic shifting drivetrain may also be an option. These systems replace traditional cable-actuated shifting with battery-powered motors to move the chain from one gear to the next. Most replace the cables with wires, though the SRAM eTap system is wireless.

If you're bargain hunting, know that most bike shops have storewide sales in March or April. This is a great time to buy, especially if you're looking for a common frame size (52cm to 58cm). Don't worry if frame size is a mystery to you; your friendly local shop staff will be happy to help you better understand it. You may also be able to find a discounted bike during the fall sale season, especially if you're on the tall or short side. Buying a used bike is another great option. Like cars, new bikes quickly lose value, so it's possible to get a great deal on a bike that's been ridden for only a season or two. The hitch is that you need to know what you are looking for (and looking at). If you find a bike you're interested in but aren't 100 percent sure about, ask a more experienced friend to take a look at it for you. Craigslist and eBay are both great places for the savvy shopper. Some cycling-centric Web sites also have online marketplaces that could be worth a look.

Finally, remember that the most important value is finding a bike that you want to ride, because it doesn't matter how great a deal you get if the bike ends up collecting dust in the back of your garage.

Chapter 2

FINE-TUNING YOUR ON-BIKE POSITION

You wouldn't wear shoes that were two sizes too big. You wouldn't drive a car with the seat so far forward your knees smashed against the steering wheel. And you shouldn't ride a bike that doesn't fit you properly. Besides being uncomfortable, an improperly fitted bike can lead to injury.

"What a lot of people may not realize is that you can be on the right size bike, but still not be fitted properly," explains Todd Carver, a bike fit expert who founded the bike fit company Rëtul and has more than 15 years of bike fitting experience. "Fitting takes you as an individual and looks at how you move on and off the bike. You can be on the best bike but if the saddle is just a centimeter too high you can run into problems."

Signs of improper bike fit range from uncomfortable pressure or chafing in the saddle area, to neck, shoulder, back, arm, and/or knee pain.

"The number-one mistake people make is compromising," says professional bike fitter and cycling coach Mat Steinmetz. "If their stem is too long, they'll try move the saddle forward instead of getting the right stem. But you really shouldn't compromise one fit coordinate for another."

It's also important to understand that there is no absolute answer to what the ideal bike fit is for you. "For almost everyone, there's an optimal range of what will work," adds Steinmetz. "But, for example, there is no perfect knee angle. There may be a 10-degree range that will work. So, once you're within that range, it becomes a process of self selection. Bike fit is a lot of trial and error within a range of norms."

To get you started on the path to a proper bike fit, start by following these simple position pointers. Remember that if your position needs significant adjustment, make changes little by little over several weeks to avoid shocking your body and possibly causing injury. Finally, keep in mind that these are only basic guidelines. If you go through these steps and are still having issues, it's time to make an appointment with a professional bike fitter.

Start with the right-size bike: Most bike shops will be equipped with an adjustable-fit bike that will help you narrow down your optimal frame size to one or two choices. Using this device is better than taking a bunch of test rides to figure out your size. For instance, if you don't like the saddle on a certain bike, it can skew your feelings about the bike in general. The fitting process should net a set of basic fit coordinates that include saddle height, stem length, stack and reach, and saddle fore/aft position. From here you want to choose a bike that fits you best and is set up in its optimal way. That means no giant stack of headset spacers, or a 70mm +/- 20-degree stem flipped upright. Typically the optimal configuration is 0 to 20mm of spacers and 90mm to 120mm stem that's +/- 6 degrees. Don't worry if you are unfamiliar with these terms and measurements. A professional bike fitter or the staff at your local bike shop can explain them to you. You can also refer to the book's glossary.

Arm position: Beware of road rider's rigor mortis. Keep your elbows bent and relaxed to absorb shock and prevent veering when you hit a bump. Keep your arms in line with your body, not splayed out to the side. This helps you maintain a more aerodynamic (and therefore faster) position.

Upper body/shoulders: Two operative words here: Be still. Imagine the energy wasted by rocking side to side with every pedal stroke on a 50-mile ride. You're better off using that energy for pumping power to the pedals. Also, beware of creeping forward on the saddle and hunching your back when tired. Shift to a higher gear and stand to pedal periodically to relieve saddle pressure and prevent stiffness in your hips and back.

Head and neck: Don't be the guy who plows into the rear of a parked car because your head is drooping off the end of your neck. Avoid putting your head down, especially when you're tired. Instead, periodically tilt your head side to side to stretch and relax the neck muscles.

Hands: With your hands on the handlebar tops, imagine that your fingers are so loose that you could play the piano. A white-knuckle hold on the bar is unnecessary and will produce energy-sapping muscle tension throughout the arms and shoulders. Grasp the drops for descents or high-speed riding, and rest on the brake lever hoods for relaxed cruising. On long climbs hold the top of the bar to sit upright and to open your chest for easier breathing. Change your hand position frequently to prevent finger numbness and upper-body stiffness. When standing, grasp the brake lever hoods lightly, and gently rock the bike side to side in sync with your pedal strokes. Always keep each thumb and a finger closed around the hoods or bar to prevent losing hold should you hit an unexpected bump.

Handlebar: Generally speaking, handlebar width should equal shoulder width. (Bars are commonly available in 38cm, 40cm, 42cm, and 44cm sizes.) If in doubt, err on the side of wider, which will help open your chest for easier breathing. You may also want to experiment with various amounts of drop, which is the distance from the center of the bar top to the center of the deepest part of the bend. Shallow drop bars are typically 125mm or less. From 125mm to 128mm is medium, and beyond that is a deep drop. A shallower drop makes it easier to maintain a more aero sprinting position, especially if you're not super flexible.

Brake lever position: You can move the levers up or down the curve of the bar to dial in comfort. Typically they are set so that each lever tip touches a straightedge when one is extended forward from under the flat bottom portion of the bar. You may find that moving the levers slightly up or down will improve comfort on the bike. To adjust the lever position, peel back the rubber hood and locate the clamp bolt. It may be on the side of the brake lever body, or inside the brake lever body (accessible when you hold down the lever arm). Once the bolt is loosened, you should be able to move the lever, then resecure.

Stem height: With your stem high enough (normally about an inch below the top of the saddle), you'll be more inclined to use the drops. Putting the stem lower can improve aerodynamics, but you may be less comfortable.

Stem length: The ideal measurement will vary based on your flexibility and anatomy. There is no one right answer. A good starting point is to sit comfortably on your saddle with elbows slightly bent and hands on the brake hoods. In this position, your view of the front hub should be obscured by the handlebar. If the hub appears in front of the bar or behind it, consider replacing the stem with a longer or shorter one accordingly. As you ride more and become more flexible, you may benefit from a longer stem, which can improve aerodynamics and flatten your back.

Back position: A flat back is the telltale sign of an experienced rider. The correct stem length is crucial for this—along with hip flexibility. Concentrate on rotating the top of your hips forward. Think of trying to touch the top tube with your stomach. Doing so will help you stop rounding your back.

Saddle height: There are numerous methods for determining saddle height, but you don't have to be a mathematician to know what the correct height looks like. Your knees should be slightly bent at the bottom of the pedal stroke, and, when viewed from behind, your hips should not rock while you are in a seated pedaling position.

Saddle tilt: Your saddle should be level. A slight downward tilt may be more comfortable if you're using an extreme forward position with an aero bar and elbow rests. But too much tilt causes you to slide forward and place additional weight on your arms.

Fore/aft saddle position: When you're seated comfortably in the center of the saddle with the crank arms horizontal, have a friend drop a plumb line from the front of your forward kneecap. It should touch the end of the crank arm. This indicates that you are set in the neutral position. If the plumb line falls either ahead or behind this mark, you should be able to achieve a neutral position by loosening the seat clamp and sliding the saddle fore or aft. (Be sure to recheck the tilt before retightening.) Some riders prefer the plumb line to fall a couple of centimeters behind the end of the crank arm to increase leverage in big gears. Conversely, some riders like a more forward position to improve leg speed. Once you have set the fore/aft position of the saddle, remember that if your reach to the handlebar needs adjustment, it is better to swap in a longer or shorter stem than it is to adjust fore/aft saddle position.

Rear end: By sliding rearward or forward on the saddle, you can emphasize different muscle groups. This can be useful on a long climb. Moving forward emphasizes the quadriceps muscle on the front of the thigh, while moving backward accentuates your hamstrings. Sitting in different locations may also relieve the pressure that can cause genital numbness.

Cleat position: Think of your footprints as you walk away from a swimming pool. Some of us are pigeon-toed. Others are duck-footed. To reduce the chance for knee pain or injury, strive for a cleat position that accommodates your natural foot angle. This most often is achieved by placing the pedal spindle at the ball of your foot; the ball is defined as being between your first and fifth metatarsal heads. Mark those spots on your shoe and set the cleat so the pedal spindle bisects that line. Now sit on your bike and hang your feet straight down. Your heel should barely scrape the pedal at the bottom of the stroke when the crank arm is in line with the seat tube.

A flat back, relaxed arms, and neutral foot position are all keys
to dialing in your ideal position on the bike.

Crank arm length: The trend is toward longer crank arms, which add power but may inhibit pedaling speed. In general, if your inseam is less than 29 inches, use 165-millimeter crank arms; 29 to 32 inches, 170-millimeter; 33 to 34 inches, 172.5-millimeter; and more than 34 inches, 175-millimeter. Crank arm length is measured from the center of the fixing bolt to the center of the pedal mounting hole. It's usually stamped on the back of the arm.

Get a professional bike fit: If you still don't feel comfortable on your bike after going through all these steps, consider getting a professional bike fit that will take into account dynamic measurements when you are in motion. This type of service typically costs $200 to $400, and should include a basic physical assessment, detailed post-fit report with fit coordinates, recommendations of bikes that could work for you, and at least one or two optional follow-up sessions. More important, after the fit you should expect to be more comfortable and pain-free on your bike, which in turn will help you to attain your performance goals.

Chapter 3

HOW TO HOLD YOUR HANDLEBARS

While your legs and lungs propel you down the road, it's your hands that provide critical contact points between your body and the bike (not to mention that whole steering thing). Each riding situation (climbing, sprinting, cruising the flats) is best suited to different grips, both for efficiency and comfort. Fortunately, the traditional road cycling drop bar provides an elegant, simple solution, offering five basic positions—and nearly limitless variations.

That variability also allows you to switch positions often, which can help prevent nerve compression that can cause numbness and hand fatigue. Just remember to always keep two fingers closed around the bar or brake lever hoods to prevent losing control if you hit a bump. Some cyclists also like to wear padded gloves for added comfort and to avoid losing skin if they take a tumble.

1. Both hands on top: This is the preferred grip for sustained seated climbing or when pushing hard at slower speeds. In these instances, the ability to sit more upright on the saddle and open the chest for easier breathing trumps any loss in aerodynamic efficiency. Because braking is not possible with

Both hands on the tops is typically used while climbing.

this grip, don't follow others too closely or use this hand position when riding in a pack.

Grasp the bar about 2 inches from either side of the stem. A narrower grip sacrifices leverage and control, while a wider one splays the elbows and creates drag. Keep your wrists and elbows slightly bent. Hold the bar lightly, but don't forget to keep at least two fingers closed around it. For added power, pull with one arm while pushing with the opposite leg, and then relax that arm.

When it's time to take a drink, this position helps maintain straight steering.

2. One hand on top: When removing a hand to eat, drink, or stretch, place the other hand about an inch from the stem. This is the safest position because your hand is closer to the turning axis, which in turn helps you reduce the chance for oversteering. Keep your eyes on the road ahead, scanning for any kind of obstacle that could derail your balance. Because you can't brake from this position, never use this grip when riding in a pack unless you're sitting at the rear of the group where you pose little danger to the other cyclists around you.

3. On the brake lever hoods: This is often the most relaxing hand position for riders. It's more aerodynamic than riding on the tops but still offers easy breathing—and access to your brakes. Use it for flat land cruising or when riding in a pack. It's also the best position for out-of-saddle climbing. However, you may want to avoid it when you're trying to ride fast or are going into a stiff headwind because of the aerodynamic penalty.

This is a great position when riding in a group and quick access to your brakes is mandatory.

To get in this position, place your thumbs on the inside of the brake hoods and rest one or two fingers on the levers for quick braking. Rest the center of your palms on the upper curves of the bars. Keep your elbows bent but not flared outward. When standing, close two fingers around the hoods for a firmer grip.

To prevent cocking the wrists excessively, make sure the levers are correctly positioned. You can assure this by taking a straightedge and extending it from under the flat lower portion of the bar. The straightedge should touch the tip of the lever. This bottom part of the bar should be horizontal or pointed a few degrees down toward the rear hub.

For an aero alternative to riding the drops (position 5), hold the hoods and bend your arms 90 degrees. Lower your chin toward the stem and try to achieve a flat back.

4. On the hoods with fingers split: This variation of position 3 (on the brake lever hoods) is a good way to relieve pressure from the normal weight-bearing part of the palms. It also facilitates bending the elbows to achieve a low aero position. However, it makes braking impossible, so don't use it when riding in a group.

This change-of-pace position can help relieve pressure on your palms.

Split your fingers and place your thumb and index fingers to the inside of the hoods with your remaining three fingers on the outside. Rest the center of your palms on the upper curves of the bar. Alternatively place two fingers on either side of the hoods. Lightly close each thumb and one finger around the bar. This position allows for a relatively low aero position.

5. In the drops: This is what drop bars were made for—and it's the most aerodynamic position for fast flat land riding and descending. It's also good for short, powerful, out-of-saddle efforts such as sprinting or pushing over

When it's time to sprint get in the drops and hammer.

the top of a small hill. Most riders find this position to be uncomfortable for long periods of time, and it doesn't provide much climbing leverage. Use this position at least a few times on every ride, however, to develop the requisite flexibility and arm strength.

Rest the edge of your hands (below the pinkie) on the flat portion of the bar with your wrists straight. Keep your elbows bent and in line with your body. When riding in a pack, descending, or cornering, keep one or two fingers on the brake levers for quick braking. During hard solo efforts, bend your arms more to get lower, but keep your head up as outlined in Chapter 2.

Hand size can be accommodated by bars with different drops, which is the measure of the distance from the center of the bar top to the center of the flat bottom portion. A drop of 125mm or less is considered shallow; 125mm to 128mm is medium; more than that is a deep drop.

Chapter 4

HOW TO DRESS FOR ANY WEATHER

No, this is not a repeat of any lessons you might have learned in the first grade. But dressing for cycling is not as simple as you'd think. Too much, too little, or just the wrong attire can wreck a ride, leaving you freezing cold or overheated and drenched in sweat. The good news is that if you know how to dress and have the right combination of gear, it's possible to ride in relative comfort in almost any type of weather.

First, a little background. Despite what you may think about your own pedaling performance, cyclists are only about 20 percent efficient, meaning if you're cranking out 200 watts, about 800 watts of heat are being produced at the same time. According to Andrew Hammond, cycling apparel brand manager at Pearl Izumi, managing this "wasted energy" is the key to staying comfortable on the bike.

"When you're pushing hard, your core temperature will rise even when your perception is that you're getting cold," says Hammond. That means having a warm core temperature doesn't necessarily equate to being comfortable on the bike. Instead, it's your skin temperature (and how wet or dry it is) that's going to affect how you feel.

Managing moisture is the key to staying warm in cold weather and cool in hot weather. This is because sweat (water + salt) is a conductive bridge between your skin and the surface of your gear. In some cases, skin exposed to cold air can cause your body to direct blood flow away from your extremities, so keeping your fingers warm may be just as much about covering your forearms as wearing the right gloves.

This is why flexibility is key. Rarely will you be perfectly comfortable for the duration of your ride, especially on cooler days, wearing exactly what you started in. Changes in effort, speed, terrain, and even climate are commonplace. So choose pieces that can be layered. Layering with arm warmers, leg warmers, caps, and vests allows you to quickly adapt to changing conditions on the road. When building a cycling wardrobe, these pieces should be among the first you purchase after you cover the basics. See Chapters 40 and 42 for more information about riding in cold weather.

Once you have the right cycling apparel, you need to know how to use them. Again, this may sound simple but there is a strategy here. Start with the layer that touches the skin. Proper layering begins with this base layer. Base layer fabrics are engineered to move moisture off your skin, helping you manage the conductive bridge to the outside world created by sweat. In cold weather, breaking this bridge by rapidly moving sweat through a base layer and into the mid or outer layer maintains the insulating properties of your other gear. And when rapidly sweating in hot weather, the movement of sweat off your skin carries heat away, which helps keep you cool.

For hot weather riding, choose an open-mesh-style base layer. The open design results in more direct airflow to the skin, helping to keep you cooler. For cool or cold conditions, opt for a piece that has slightly more dense fabric.

Next, pull on your main upper-body layer, typically a jersey. No matter what conditions in which you're riding, it's critical to select a second layer that is designed to keep you dry. With that in mind, priorities change depending on conditions.

On balmy days, again choose a more open mesh fabric to maintain some direct airflow to the skin. If it's just warm, focus on the moisture transfer benefits of the fabric. For cool weather, chose a thermal layer to trap warm air next to your body. And when it's truly cold out, opt for a softshell layer that can be used alone or with a transfer middle layer. This provides protection from the elements, warmth, and moisture management.

Moving downward, it's time to address your lower body. Unlike the upper body, typically only one (if any) layer is worn on the legs. In cool conditions, the two priorities are comfort and knee protection, meaning knee warmers.

For hot or warm conditions, opt for bib shorts made from fabrics with cooling and moisture-transferring properties.

Knee coverage is important in cool or cold temperatures. Here, there are typically two camps. Some cyclists prefer bib shorts with knee warmers, while others opt for lightweight tights. Shorts with warmers offer more versatility should the conditions warm up. When it's truly cold, though, you'll want a softshell tight or thermal full-length leg warmers combined with thermal bib shorts. Again, see Chapters 40 and 42 for riding in cold weather.

Within this conversation, it's also important to consider the actual weather elements. Protecting yourself against wind and water are key to staying comfortable on the bike.

On windy days, a vest is one of the easiest ways to stay warm, especially on descents or when the temperature drops. Look for a vest that fits properly. It should not flap around or interfere with how you handle the bike. Lightweight packable jackets are another good option. Also consider using a lightweight shoe cover to keep your feet warm.

If it's raining (or even if there's a chance of rain), having a waterproof barrier is key. These jackets typically have taped seams and are truly waterproof. But if the chance of rain is slim or short-lived, you can probably get away with a light rain jacket with standard water resistance. These lightweight jackets are usually more packable for storage in jersey pockets. See Chapter 41 for more information on riding in the rain.

Part Two

SKILL BUILDING 101

Chapter 5

FINDING YOUR FLOW IN TRAFFIC

Before getting into the technical details of how to (and not to) ride your bike, it's critical that you first understand the most basic of cycling skills: How to avoid getting hit by a car while riding your bike. Of course, there's no guarantee in this game, no matter how diligent and cautious you are. But by following some general guidelines, you can dramatically increase your odds of having a fun—and safe—ride.

The number-one safety precaution happens before you ever roll away from home: Wear a helmet. Every time you ride, for the entire duration of your ride. Even if you're just rolling down the street to grab a coffee, wear a brain protector. Set an example when you're cruising around the block with your kids and protect your noggin. There is no excuse not to wear a helmet whenever you ride. Today's helmets are wispy light and make a huge difference in the outcome of an accident. Got it? Good.

Now, let's discuss what to do once you roll away from home—with your helmet on, of course.

Don't be that guy: We have all seen cyclists who wander across the road, hopscotch between the sidewalk and the street, and/or weave between parked cars. It is extremely difficult to tell what these riders will do next. Pedestrians jump back. Drivers slam on their brakes. Other cyclists shake their heads, knowing that these numbskulls are giving the rest of us a bad name.

Fortunately, we've also seen cyclists who blend gracefully into the flow of traffic. You always know where they are headed and you feel comfortable around them, whether you're on a bicycle, in a car, or on foot. They make riding look easy. The following tips will help you to be like them—not the other guys.

With few exceptions, the safest way to ride in traffic is to act like the surrounding vehicular traffic and follow its normal flow. Cyclists who ride this way get where they're going faster and are less likely to end up in an accident.

Generally, the more you follow normal traffic patterns, the more predictable and safer you are. The rules of the road establish a way to behave in every situation. Sometimes a cyclist has to wait for drivers at a stop sign, for example, but sometimes it's the drivers who have to wait. The rules of the road protect you by making it clear how every vehicle should behave in a given circumstance.

Safe riding begins with riding on the right. Unknowing cyclists think that they are safer on the left, where they can see cars coming toward them. But riding on the left is one of the primary causes of accidents. If you ride in violation of this basic traffic rule, you greatly increase your risk of an accident. You also give up all your rights. If you are on the left and an accident occurs, a court will almost always find you at fault.

Keep in mind that a head-on collision is generally more difficult to avoid, and the effects from the impact are more severe than if both participants are traveling in the same direction. If you ride against the flow of traffic, you and an oncoming car approach each other at the sum of your respective speeds. If you are going 15 miles per hour and the car is going 35 miles per hour, the closing speed is 50 miles per hour. But if you are riding on the right with the flow of traffic, the difference in speed is only 20 miles per hour. That means a driver behind you has much more time to react.

By riding on the right, drivers and pedestrians about to emerge from side streets and crosswalks will be looking toward you, in the direction traffic normally comes from.

Live on the edge: Normally, slower traffic keeps to the right, and faster traffic passes on the left. Because your bicycle is slower than passing cars, it's best to ride near the right edge of the road.

The usable width of the road begins where you can ride without increased danger. If a road has a gravel shoulder, its edge is covered with sand or trash, or the pavement is all busted up, don't ride there. You will usually find better pavement about 12 to 18 inches to the left of the road edge where it's swept clean of sand and debris by passing traffic. Thus, for a cyclist, the right edge of the road begins here.

Most bicycle accidents are simple falls due to either rider error or encounters with road hazards. Train your eyes to scan the scene ahead. Look up at traffic and down at the road for potholes and debris.

Where there are parked cars, the usable width of the street begins about 3 feet to the left of them. The same goes for a wall, hedge, or other type of obstruction. Ride far enough into the lane to avoid creating blind spots. If you ride too close to parked cars on your right, you can't see around them into side streets and driveways. A pedestrian, car, or bike could come out from between them; drivers on side streets might nose their cars into your path to check for traffic; or the door of a parked car could swing open in front of you. As you approach a blind intersection or driveway, you should be even farther from the road edge. Imagine the front of a car suddenly protruding into your path. Avoid this danger zone.

Don't dart into the spaces between parked cars. If you weave to the right after passing a parked car, it will hide you from drivers approaching from behind. Then you have to pop back out when you reach the next parked car. Picture yourself in the place of a driver a couple of hundred feet behind you. Could this driver see you before you suddenly reappear?

Remember that at speeds above 5 miles per hour, you can't stop in time to avoid a car door. Your only choice is to swerve into the street, which could put you into the path of a passing car. Most motorists don't mind slowing for a competent, predictable cyclist. But drivers might become enraged if they have to slam the brakes for a rider who suddenly swerves in front of them.

Find your safe spot: If the road has a paved shoulder or an extra-wide right lane, don't ride all the way over at the right edge. Instead, follow a straight line 3 to 4 feet to the right of the cars in the right lane. Stay a constant distance from the painted line that marks the boundary of the right lane.

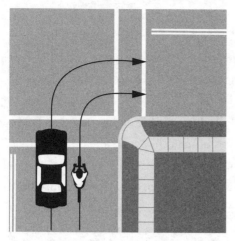

By moving away from the right edge you leave yourself room to turn out of the way if a car cuts you off.

If you ride at the far right edge of the shoulder, you're much more likely to be cut off by a right-turning car. If this should happen, it's harder for you to avoid an accident. By the time you see the car, it will be blocking your path. If you're closer to the car, you can turn with it and avoid hitting its side.

Conversely, if the lane is narrow, cars must move partway into the opposing lane to pass you. Thus, on a narrow two-lane road, stay alert for strings of cars coming at you in case one suddenly pulls into your lane to pass. Ride near the right edge if cars are coming from only one direction at a time; then cars from the rear can get around you without having to move too far into the other lane.

When necessary, take control: If cars are coming from both directions, you have to take control of the situation. You can't risk letting a driver pass you in the face of oncoming traffic. There's simply no room. Glance behind then take the first opportunity to move to the middle of your lane.

Try to merge to the middle of a narrow right lane for a blind curve, where there might be oncoming traffic. This makes you visible earlier to drivers coming from behind. They will have to slow and follow you. Since you can see farther ahead, it helps to communicate with the driver behind you by making a "slow" signal (left arm extended downward, open hand facing the rear). This indicates that you're aware of the car behind and that it's unsafe to pass. Don't let an impatient driver cause an accident.

Understand that the law is on your side. You have the same right to use the road as a motorist, and this sometimes means making other traffic slow down for you. Because you don't have eyes in the back of your head, you can't be expected to keep track of the traffic behind you. The driver approaching from the rear is required to slow and follow if it's not possible to pass safely.

It may seem dangerous to make a car slow for you, but it's actually not. The usual reason cyclists feel unsafe on narrow roads is that they don't take control of the situation. Remember that the drivers behind you don't have room to pass safely anyway. If you ride along the right edge, you're inviting them to try, which may result in you being squeezed off the road. If you clearly show that it's not safe for drivers to pass, it's unlikely that they will.

When it becomes safe to pass, give the driver a wave-by signal. If conditions are causing you to block traffic for more than a short time, consider pulling off and let the faster moving traffic roll past. It's the same behavior you'd expect of a driver of a slow-moving RV on a busy road.

On a road with two or more narrow lanes in your direction (like many city streets), you should ride in the middle of the right lane. Make drivers move to the passing lane to get by you. If you ride along the right edge, two cars may pass you simultaneously side by side, which is a dangerous situation for you and the drivers.

Act like a car: Usually, cars travel faster than bicycles, but not always. Perhaps a row of cars has slowed because of congestion. Or maybe you're riding down a hill as fast as the traffic flow.

If you're going the same speed, pull into line with the cars. When riding down a hill at high speed, you need more room to steer and brake. Besides, it's dangerous to ride beside a car. If the driver is unaware you're there, he or she could turn right or squeeze you into the curb.

As long as you can keep up with the car in front, stay in line with it. If you begin to fall behind, pull to the right. If you want to pass, do it on the left, just as if you were driving a car. First, look back for traffic to make sure that you can pull safely into the passing lane. Signal your intention by extending your left arm. Keep your distance from the side of the car. Put yourself in a place where the driver will look for you.

If you're passing a big truck or bus, use even more clearance (5 to 6 feet) because it could move over before you can get out of its way. When your pass is complete and it's clear to return to the right lane, signal by extending your right arm and move back into the right lane.

Sometimes the vehicle that you're passing will pick up speed while you're still next to it. If this happens, maintain your position in the lane and brake lightly, if necessary, to fall back. Wait for an opening, then signal and merge to your normal position in the right lane.

A cyclist's place on the road follows accepted rules just as it does for motorists. Stay to the right when moving slowly, pull to the left to pass. The way you carry out these rules is a little different because your bicycle is narrow and usually slower than a motorized vehicle. Now that you know how, you're ready to blend smoothly and safely into the traffic flow.

Chapter 6

SMOOTH SPINNING

Talented riders make cycling look easy. While mere mortals labor when the pace ramps up or the road tilts skyward, these titans on two wheels spin along with an almost casual cadence. Yes, genetic ability plays a role. The Eddy Merckxes of this world are born, not made. But no matter your birth-given abilities, how you pedal affects your bike riding. The smoother you propel the drivetrain, the more relaxed and stable your upper body becomes. The more motion there is in your upper body, the less efficient you'll be. Indeed, pedaling is an art, an art that is definitely lost on some.

Truth is, there is a proper technique that produces a smooth pedaling style, which is typically expressed in the well-worn phrase "pedal in circles." Indeed, if you are just pressing down at the top of the pedal stroke—and not applying force during the full 360-degress of rotation—you are not pedaling efficiently.

Decades ago, packs of wool-jersey-clad cyclists would do early-season, low-gear miles. The idea was to first develop and refine form and then worry about speed and fitness. In winter these practitioners of perfect pedaling rode stationary rollers, which put a premium on pedaling style, not to mention overall balance. On rollers, even a brief lapse in concentration or uneven, erratic pedaling can result in a flop to the floor.

You'll also occasionally hear true cycling aficionados talk about *souplesse,* French for suppleness. In the two-wheeled world, a rider with souplesse is a stylish rider with a smooth, easy pedaling style. There is no wasted upper body motion, no squirming on the saddle. Just the perfectly steady spin of legs, and ankles and feet, effortlessly propelling the bike down the road.

BECOMING SMOOTH

Among the best ways to achieve more fluidity in your pedal stroke are one-legged drills and riding a fixed-gear bike. One-legged pedaling forces you to pedal all the way through the stroke and develop your muscles accordingly. Whether you do this outside or inside on a trainer, try to make it a regular component of your off-season training. Start with 20 revolutions per side and increase to several minutes at a stretch. Repeat two to five times per ride for each leg.

Opt for a relatively tall gear, something in the area of the 53 × 13, which will help slow down the motion and really allow you to focus on your form. The idea is to eliminate the dead spot in your pedal stroke. The bottom of your stroke should mimic the motion of scraping mud off the bottom of your shoe. At the top of the stroke, think about driving your toes and knees forward. Remember that you want to keep your toes relaxed at all times. Resist curling them up or clinching the sole of your shoe.

For an even more intense training session, consider jumping on a fixed gear bike, which behaves sort of like the tricycle you probably rode as a child. If the bike is moving, the pedals are moving, too. There's no coasting—and that's the magic. Because you are stuck in one gear and must constantly pedal, you are forced to smooth out your stroke. If not, you'll get bounced around on the saddle—especially going downhill.

Decades ago, serious cyclists would ride a fixed gear for the first 1,000 or so miles of each season, reacquainting their muscles with the smooth, round pedal stroke. Use whatever training technique is best for you, but keep in mind that riding a fixed gear bike is a bad idea in hilly terrain. Because you can't gear down when climbing, you will probably push too large a gear when going uphill. This can put undue stress on your knees, which can lead to injury. Going downhill on a fixed gear bike can be downright terrifying because the bike (and pedals) will want to spin faster than your legs are capable of turning.

It's also possible to improve the smoothness of your spin by riding in a small gear and pedaling through the downhills. It's not easy to keep up with the gear when moving fast, meaning you'll be pedaling at a very high cadence, even up to the range of 150 revolutions per minute (rpm). At first you may feel as if you're going to bounce right out of your shoes. But if you relax and spin, your pedal stroke will become smoother over time.

Though it's difficult if not impossible to apply positive force all the way through the pedal stroke, it's important to at least have the perception of constant pressure all the way around. To help facilitate the motion, try installing a mirror next to your indoor trainer and watch yourself.

It's also good practice to keep your upper body as motionless as possible. One good exercise involves riding up a long, gradual hill in a big gear. If the grade is around 5 percent, then a gear along the lines of a 53 × 15 is a good one to use. At first, ride for only a minute or so. Then build up to several 5-minute repetitions per workout. Strive for as little body and arm motion as possible and stay in the saddle. Like one-legged pedaling, this gives you a feel for a complete, round stroke. It's like weight lifting on the bike.

This drill is not suitable for anyone with bad knees, and it can lead to poor habits if done to the point of sloppiness (when you start twisting and lurching). In other words, don't try it unless you already have a good base of fitness and your knees can handle it.

Bottom line: Improving your pedal stroke is an important part of becoming a better cyclist and should therefore be part of your training program. Here are some more tips and tricks that will help you smooth out your pedal stroke.

Scrape your foot: When on your bike, think about pulling your foot back and up as if you were scraping something off the bottom of your shoe. You should feel tension in your hamstrings, and when the pedal is lifting up the feeling should be one of lifting your knee with an assist from your hip flexors.

Smooth it out: Try to eliminate surges in your pedal stroke by focusing on just the second half of the rotation, when your foot is coming up.

Push your foot forward: Focus on pushing your foot forward in your shoe, touching your toes to the front of your shoe when you're at the top of the pedal stroke. This helps you transition through the 12 o'clock position, which is a dead spot in a pedal stroke. Start out in an easy gear and ramp up resistance as your technique improves.

Lift your feet: When pedaling out of the saddle, think about lifting your feet during the upstroke by pulling up with your hamstrings.

Set your saddle: Finally, make sure your saddle is set at the proper height. If it's too high, you'll rock back and forth. If it's too low, you'll put undue stress on your knees. To determine proper saddle height, sit on your bike while leaning against a wall. Now drape both feet straight down. If your saddle height is set correctly, your heel should just graze the pedal when the crank arm is in the 6 o'clock position.

Chapter 7
BRAKING TECHNIQUE

Braking is one of those skills many of us learn early in our cycling careers. It often goes something like this: A young child, bombing carefree down a hill, inadvertently drifts off line toward a parked car or some other obstacle. In a moment of panic, the child tries to adjust direction and simultaneously hits the brakes a little too hard. This locks up the rear wheel, causing the bike to skid sideways. Instead of steering past the car or around the huge pothole, the child smacks into the side of the car or runs right over that pothole.

And there lies the first (and most important) lesson of proper braking technique: Don't panic. When confronted with an unexpected obstacle, respond in a calm and calculated way. If you panic, you too may smack into the side of a car or nail that pothole.

Although you'll ride most often with your hands on the brake hoods, maximum control is attained while in the drops of your handlebars. Just watch the Tour de France pros. When going downhill fast, they put their hands in the drops with one finger extended to each brake lever. This makes it easier to feather the brakes, the cycling equivalent of lightly pumping the brakes on your car. More fingers around the handlebar means a better grip. Modern brakes (especially hydraulic disc brakes, which are showing up on more and more road bikes) work effectively with the strength of just one finger.

If you ride a lot, you'll soon learn that pulling the brake lever too hard is often the cause of accidents. When you grab the lever quickly with full force, the likely result is often skidding and a loss of control (remember our wayward child). Instead, try a gentle squeeze using just one or two fingers. Equipment setup is also important. Make sure you can reach the levers. Most modern brake levers have reach-adjust functionality, so if the brake lever is too close or too far away you can move it accordingly.

Make sure the levers are working properly. If using a traditional cable-actuated rim brake, keep the brake cables and pivot points lubed and moving freely. The cable housing should run relatively straight (no kinks). Also, check that the pads strike the rim at the same time. If they are out of alignment, they'll pull the wheel, which can adversely affect steering.

If you're using hydraulic disc brakes, make sure your brake pads are not worn out. You'll also occasionally need to bleed your brakes, which is the process of purging air from your brake lines. (Unless you really know what you are doing, this is a task best left to an experienced bike shop mechanic.) You'll know it's time when the lever action starts to feel mushy or the lever pulls all the way to the bar without producing adequate braking force. Brake failure is nothing to mess around with, so get your bike to the shop right away if you have even the slightest doubt about your bike's brakes.

HANDLING TURNS

Proper braking techniques allow you to safely negotiate upcoming turns. When you enter a corner, you should have already slowed down so that you don't have to apply the brakes while turning. As you approach the corner apply both brakes evenly, while at the same time establishing your line. By the apex of the turn you should be off the brakes completely and in control so that you can carry speed out of the turn. Also make sure to keep your weight back. Braking tends to push you forward, loading the front wheel and making maneuvering more difficult.

Keep in mind the harder you brake while in a turn, the more upright your bike wants to be. And the more upright it is, the less it wants to turn. This has important implications when you enter a turn with too much speed and attempt to slow down rapidly. Instead of panicking and pulling hard on the brakes, try to feather them so that you don't lock up your wheels. Otherwise you may end up skidding into the lane of oncoming traffic.

Many riders mistakenly think that the front brake should never be used alone, but in actuality a light touch can help keep your bike in control. Of course too much front brake can wash the bike out from under you. So don't be afraid to use the front brake, but do so deftly.

Chapter 8

IMPROVE YOUR CORNERING TECHNIQUE

If you want to go fast on your bike, you need to learn how to corner. Whether it's racing a criterium or bombing down a long mountain descent, the ability to maintain speed while safely navigating your way through twists and turns is integral to cycling. You will quickly find out that some riders are simply better than others when it comes to taking corners.

There are those who make it look easy, as they arc a smooth and confident path down the road. But make no mistake about it, proper cornering technique on a bicycle is a skill that is learned, practiced, and maybe someday perfected.

Generally speaking, you can break down cornering into the following three styles, based on the correlation of your body to the bike and the differing angles of lean for both your bike and body. If you learn the mechanics of these styles, your riding will be safer and more fun—and you will go faster.

UPRIGHT STEERING

Upright steering operates on the idea that the more upright your bike is, the less chance it will slide out from under you when cornering. In essence, you try to keep your bike as upright as possible and corner by simply turning the handlebar like the steering wheel of a car.

This technique works well in certain conditions, such as when the pavement is slippery from moisture, oil, or gravel. It's prudent to keep the bike vertical and steer it over the slick stuff at a slower (and thereby safer) speed. This keeps sideways force to a minimum and directs traction downward.

However, when a bike is upright it has a hard time turning at speeds much above 15 miles per hour, which is pretty slow in most instances. That's why upright steering is typically the least effective method of turning. It makes you top heavy, and modifying your line is virtually impossible once you have committed to the turn.

INCLINATION

At faster speeds—and especially through shallow turns—your bike will make a safe, wide arc if you just lean over and trust it. This is called inclination, and it's the most common method of cornering. Nothing fancy here. It is just a matter of leaning your body and bike together and following the natural line through the turn. You really don't need to do anything but put weight on your outside pedal, which should be at the 6 o'clock, or down, position, and lean with the bike as much as needed to accomplish the turn.

The hitch here is that a certain amount of trial and error is required to figure out how much lean is required at certain speeds through different turns. When in unfamiliar territory, only use this method through consistent, softly arcing turns where you can clearly see the exit. You also need faith that your tires won't slide out if you lean too far.

COUNTERSTEERING

Countersteering is arguably the best steering method because it's the quickest way to get the bike through a turn, yet it still allows you to make corrections while leaning. To understand countersteering, ride along a straight road or parking lot with no traffic, get into the drops, and as the speed builds, quickly press down with your left hand. The bike heels left, then veers right. The reason this happens is that at speed a bike wants to turn when angled, and the easiest way to angle it is to lever the front wheel over by pushing the handlebar away from the direction you want to turn.

Skeptical? Try it. Push the bar away from the turn and your bike will nod in the direction you push, then quickly dive toward the opposite side and into the turn. As you get more comfortable, try keeping your hands in the drops. Then weight the outside pedal, let your inside knee point into the turn, and straighten your inside arm as you push that side of the handlebar down, not with the quick punch that initiated the countersteer, but with continual pressure.

Should you come upon something unexpected while turning, then the beauty of countersteering should become clear. You will discover that you can change your line instantly by either putting more pressure on the inside of the handlebar (which tightens your turn radius) or pulling the bike upright underneath you (which broadens the radius). Just remember that bringing the bike upright decreases your ability to get around the turn. So once you're past the obstacle, you'll need to push the inside bar down and continue turning.

Staying loose and relaxed on the bike allows you to move around and subtly influence its line through the turn. As the bike banks, your body naturally centers itself in juxtaposition to the angle of the bike. Alpine skiers understand this technique as angulation, the process of staying centered over the main part of your mass while making turns.

When passing through a corner, look about 8 to 10 feet ahead
at where you want to go.

Cornering Tips from the Experts

Don't max out your tire pressure of your road bike, advises Jeremy Powers, multitime US national cyclocross champion. "Just because you can put 120 psi in your tires doesn't mean you should," he adds. "If you are running 23c or 25c road tires with tubes, 90 psi is a good starting place. If your tires are wider than that or if you are running a tubeless setup, you can go even lower. The lower pressure will result in a more comfortable ride, and put more tire on the pavement, which increases traction." Powers also says that it's important to look where you want to go. "The bike has an uncanny way of following your eyes," he says. "So, you want to look through the corner about 8 to 10 feet ahead. And don't stare at the big pothole in the middle of the road or you'll likely end up going right over it."

Follow your fast friends, says Scott Moninger, former pro racer-turned-coach. "When I raced in Europe, I would always try to get on the back wheel of the best descenders," recalls Moninger. "The thinking was that if that person can make it through the corner and keep their bike upright, then I should be able, too. Use that person as a gauge to calculate speed, and get set up to go through the turn."

It's simple: Practice, advises cycling coach Frank Overton, owner and founder of FasCat Coaching in Boulder, Colorado. "Do it over and over again, trying to go a little faster each time," he says. "Like a lot of things, cornering is a skill, so just like taking batting practice or hitting golf balls at the driving range, the more you do it, the better you will get."

Finally, know that descending and braking tend to push your body forward, which loads the front wheel. Counteract this by pushing back on the saddle and flattening your upper body along the length of the bike to get better weight distribution. Practice these techniques and you'll soon be diving in and out of corners like the pros.

Chapter 9

HOW TO DESCEND LIKE A PRO

Unless you do all your pedaling on the flatlands of Kansas, at some point you're going to have to go downhill on your road bike. And often those downhills involve tight turns. At first, the notion of zipping through switchbacks may be a little scary. But, with practice, you'll soon embrace one of cycling's great rewards, comfortably slicing in and out of turns as you speed downhill.

As is often the case in road cycling, going downhill often starts with an uphill effort. But before you begin a descent, take care not to end the hill climb too soon. Many riders ease up when they reach the crest of a hill. It's a natural response when muscles are tired and breathing is labored. But assuming you plan on continuing down the road, you're losing valuable momentum by easing up too soon during the transition from climbing to descending. Instead, keep pedaling over the top until gravity takes hold and you're able to start shifting to higher gears. Once you've picked up speed, soft-pedal to let your muscles recover. By not easing up at the end of each climb, you'll become faster on hilly terrain.

Once headed downhill, be especially cautious if you do not have intimate familiarity with the descent. Regardless, any number of hazards may be around the next bend: gravel, sand, vehicles, driveways, animals, broken pavement, even a stop sign at a busy intersection. Temper your speed by feathering the brakes with one finger on each lever. Keep your weight back, but sit up to let more air catch your chest. As we learned in the last chapter, apply the brakes before entering a turn.

If you're riding with someone who knows the descent, jump on their wheel and follow their line. Just make sure to hang back several lengths in case something goes wrong. There's minimal drafting benefit from following right on someone's wheel while descending.

Remember to always look ahead to see what's coming and focus on looking where you want to go. Your wheels tend to track where you look, so don't stare at the pothole you're trying to avoid. Instead, focus on the clear path beside it. Like magic, that's where your bike will go.

Traffic permitting, use the entire lane; so this will allow you to make a wider turn, which translates into less risk of your bike sliding out. Enter the turn wide and aim for the apex of the corner, pointing toward the outside of the lane as you exit the turn. This makes the corner as wide and fast as possible. Just remember that unless you are riding in a closed-road situation, there may be a car around the corner. Stay alert, and always stay in your lane.

Now that we've covered the basics, here are some other tips and techniques to ensure that your descents are fun and safe.

➤ It's not necessary to keep a low, streamlined position while descending. By sitting up with your hands on the brake hoods, you can see better. You'll also breathe easier, which will help you recover from the climb. Most riders don't find it difficult to brake effectively from the top of the brake levers.

➤ Wear sunglasses to protect your eyes from bugs or other airborne objects that may cause injury. Shades will also stop cold air that could make your eyes water. If you suddenly can't see while on a fast, curvy descent, things can get ugly fast.

➤ Descend in a high gear, but not necessarily the highest. You may need to pedal through a flatter section or two on the way down. Even when rolling too fast to pedal, revolve your legs slowly to prevent muscles from tightening and cramping.

➤ If hard braking is necessary, apply both brakes simultaneously. The front has more power because your weight is moving forward, but using it without the rear can make the bike hard to control. Using the rear brake alone can cause the rear wheel to lock up and skid.

➤ Do the majority of your braking before you enter the turn. Braking while turning can reduce tire grip.

➤ Don't stand, but don't sit. Instead hover over your saddle for better balance and control.

➤ When coasting, keep the crank arms horizontal. In this position, your feet help your arms and butt support your body weight and absorb road shock. As you enter each turn, place the outside pedal down and press hard on it.

➤ Try the countersteering technique discussed in Chapter 8. Extend your torso to the outside of the turn while pushing the handlebar down to the inside. This accentuates the turning effect while actually decreasing the chance of skidding.

➤ When exiting the corner, give a few hard pedal strokes. This will help you slingshot out of the turn and get you back up to speed.

➤ Above all, stay relaxed. Once these techniques are ingrained, your bike should feel as if it's flowing down the hill like water. It's hard to beat the excitement of fast, yet safe, descending. Soon, you will be searching for climbs because of the fun that's on the other side.

Chapter 10

HOW TO RIDE SAFELY IN A GROUP

Group rides are a great way to boost fitness, make new friends, and explore unfamiliar territory. Typically these rides meet at the same place and time each week, then roll out on a predetermined route. Some rides will be chatty and social, others full-on race pace hammerfests.

Don't be surprised if your first group ride is a tad intimidating. It is sort of like the first day of school. You don't know anyone and you don't know what to expect. The good news is that cyclists are generally a friendly bunch, so it won't be long before you are making friends. Here are key tips to follow to make your group ride experience fun and safe.

Do some research: Before showing up to a group, find out what it is all about. Good sources of info include your neighborhood bike shop, local cycling club and team Web sites, and of course social media. Find out the meeting time, meeting place, approximate ride distance, and typical pace. That way you will come ready to hammer hard—or just roll along at a casual pace.

Say hello: When you roll up to the meeting spot, introduce yourself. It is a great way to break the ice, and it will help you get the basic gist on the ride and riders. If you do not know the area, let someone know. That way if you get dropped, they might wait for you, or at least point you back toward home. As a precautionary measure, bring a GPS or smartphone in case you end up alone and lost.

Ask questions: Most cyclists welcome the opportunity to share expertise, so don't be afraid to ask for insights on the ride. The more you learn, the more confident you will become and the more fun you will have riding with the group.

Recognize the flow: Most group rides employ either a two-up or rotating pace line. Determine protocol in your group and then follow along. Two-up pace lines are when the group rides double-file, with the front pair of riders sharing the workload of breaking the wind for a few minutes at a time, and then pulling off to let the next pair come forward. When it is your turn to pull, keep the speed steady. Don't accelerate suddenly. Also make sure not to ride with your front wheel ahead of your partner. This is known as half-wheeling and may force your partner to ride harder than they want to. When your time at the front is over, alert your partner that you are pulling off, then move to the outside of the line and slide to the back of the group.

Some group rides start with a two-up pace line and a more casual pace, and then transition to a rotating pace line as the speed picks up. In a rotating pace line, each rider takes a brief pull alone at the front and then drifts back into the draft. The group is essentially in a circular motion. This allows the group to maintain a faster pace. When it is your turn to pull, keep the pace steady, then move over to the return line. Take care to leave enough room so that your rear wheel is safely clear of the front wheel of the person who pulled off ahead of you (they will be behind you now). Once you are safely in the return line, ease up a little so the next person pulling through does not have to accelerate to get around you.

Keep it steady: Ever notice how easy some cyclists are to ride behind? Their path on the road seems drawn by a draftsman's tools, and their tempo has the steadiness of an electric motor. So how does one become such a paragon of predictability? The first step is to understand that you are responsible for the rider(s) behind you. This means you can speed them up, slow them down, or even make them crash.

One great trick is to visualize a string tied between your saddle and the following rider's handlebar. Imagine that sudden accelerations will break this string, leaving your friend behind. Conversely, quick stops will make the string go slack, causing the rider behind to overlap your wheel—and likely crash. Your job is to keep the string taut. This doesn't necessarily mean maintaining the same speed all the time. Instead, concentrate on exerting the same pedal pressure.

Also remember that just touching your brakes while riding at the front can cause problems behind you. Instead, feather your brakes and continue pedaling. This moderates speed without the sort of abrupt change that can derail trailing riders. If you do need to brake hard, call out "stopping" or "slowing" so that others know what's going on and can react accordingly. Another way to control speed without braking is to move your body into a broader, more open position and let the wind slow you.

Do not surge: Whenever you are sharing the workload by alternating the front position, do not surge. If you have a GPS or other speed-measuring device mounted on your bike, check your speed before you get to the front, and then try to maintain that same speed as you pull through. Once you have done your time, look over your shoulder for traffic, then pull off without accelerating. Slow a bit so that you can drift to the back of the group. Keep pedaling while you are doing this, and only swing out as far as necessary to clear the group (about a handlebar width). Take care to hold a steady line and tempo when reaching for a jersey pocket or a water bottle. Even better, wait until you are at the back of the group—this is usually the safest place to eat or take a swig.

Hold your line: Imagine you are riding on rails, even if this occasionally means going over a bump that you would otherwise swerve to avoid. Same goes for bunny hopping obstacles. Save this move for when you are riding alone or have plenty of distance between yourself and others.

If a larger obstacle such as a parked car or giant pothole is coming up, give both verbal and hand warnings. While on the front, you are the de facto group leader, and it is your job to scan the road and call out (and point out) obstacles. When cornering at the front of a group, follow the expected line. This means starting wide, gradually cutting to the apex, then swinging wide again.

Use hand signals: Give notice of an upcoming turn by sticking your arm out and pointing directly toward whichever way you are headed. If the group is large, complement these hand gestures with a loud shout out: "left turn" or "right turn" or the like. Other riders in the group should help telegraph that information through to the back end of the bunch.

Close but not too close: When riding in a group, never overlap wheels with the rider in front of you. Instead, stay at least 6 to 12 inches behind. Try to avoid freewheel fixation, where you become mesmerized by staring at the wheel in front of you. Instead, look ahead at the lead riders and beyond, scanning for trouble.

Call out cars: When following other riders, announce all overtaking vehicles, especially if one of your fellow riders has drifted out into the road. A loud and clear "car back" will let those ahead know that it is time to tuck in so the car can pass safely. When leading other riders, vehicle traffic ahead (stopped, slow moving, and especially oncoming) should be identified with a loud "car up." This same idea applies to crossing through intersections. Riders at the front should yell out "clear" when it's safe to pass through.

Climb, don't kick: One common new-rider faux pas is "drop kicking" the rider behind you at the start of a climb. This happens because cadence naturally decreases as you rise from the saddle, causing your bike to momentarily slow down. The trailing rider may then hit your rear wheel and potentially topple over. This situation is often exacerbated because both riders are in oxygen debt and not in full possession of their faculties.

There is a simple way to avoid this. Before you stand up, shift to the next high gear to compensate for the slower cadence. At the same time, maintain pressure on the pedals so that your bike doesn't move backward relative to the rider behind you. This sit-stand transition often takes a little practice, but soon becomes natural. Concentrate on eliminating any freewheeling as you stand. Instead, try to always maintain pressure on the pedals. The same idea applies when you sit back down. Downshift to an easier gear and concentrate on maintaining pedal pressure to avoid an abrupt change in speed.

Chill out: Even if you are the strongest rider in the group, do not start attacking at the base of the first climb. Group rides have established rhythms and you won't make many friends if you break that rhythm. Besides, riding smart means waiting for someone else to attack, then jumping on their wheel, hiding in the draft, and then rolling away solo near the end of the climb.

Part Three

HOW TO SAFELY COMMUTE BY BIKE

Chapter 11
SAFE CITY CYCLING

There are few greater joys for a cyclist than watching car commuters lurch along in bumper-to-bumper traffic while you casually pedal home from work. Instead of adding to life's aggravations, commuting by bike melts away workday stress. Rather than spending more time sitting on your butt, you are sitting on your bike's saddle and getting a workout. And instead of contributing to the world's pollution problems, you are doing your part to make our planet a little greener and cleaner.

Need more motivation? Consider these eye-opening statistics from the cycling advocacy organization PeopleForBikes (peopleforbikes.org).

➤ Using a bicycle to commute 4 days a week for 4 miles (one-way) saves about 54 gallons of gas a year.

➤ The energy and resources needed to build one medium-size car could produce 100 bicycles.

➤ Cars and SUVs account for 40 percent of daily oil consumption in the US.

➤ Traffic congestion wastes 2 billion gallons of gas a year.

➤ It costs about $50 to build and maintain one space in a bike rack and $500 for a bike locker, yet one car parking space in a parking structure costs about $8,500.

Despite those compelling statistics, many cyclists hate riding in traffic. Indeed, safety concerns while riding in traffic consistently rank as one of the top reasons people don't commute by bicycle more often. And frankly it's understandable. Traffic, especially in big cities, can be downright scary when you're on a bicycle. Motorists speed by in cars the size of tanks. Pedestrians blindly walk into your path. And all the while, you're trying to navigate roadways that are often littered with cracks, potholes, and who knows what.

While you can't change any of these factors, you can alter your reaction to them by learning how to ride more safely and smoothly in even the worst rush-hour traffic. Here are some fundamental tips that will help you build your confidence and skills.

Practice makes better: Pedal between parked cars at malls or supermarkets to get used to having all that metal around you. This will help you feel comfortable when drivers simply pass normally. Save your adrenaline for true emergencies.

Look where you want to go: Don't spend too much time worrying about the traffic behind you. The majority of accidents involving cars and bikes happen when the driver and rider cross each other's path at intersections and driveways, especially when a driver turns in front of a rider.

Make eye contact: Never assume that a motorist sees you or that you have the right of way. And don't take a walk signal, a green traffic light, or a driver's awareness for granted. Instead, always make eye contact with drivers to ensure that they see you.

Hold your line: Keep track of what's happening behind you by mastering the skill of looking behind you without swerving. Practice riding on the painted line of a quiet road or parking lot. Once you can do this, try maintaining your course while turning your head to the left. Slightly drop your left shoulder while keeping your right shoulder level. Don't rely on peripheral vision. You should be able to turn your head far enough to see clearly behind you.

If you're struggling, try sticking out your left arm straight behind you, then turn your head, shoulders, and neck as you look over your left shoulder. Sighting down your arm will help you keep riding straight. Eventually, you'll be able to do it without using your arm as a guide.

Get noticed: The majority of drivers don't actively ignore cyclists. They are just conditioned to be on the lookout for larger obstacles (or maybe they're looking at their smartphone). For this reason, don't be overly courteous and hug the gutter if there is no bike lane or shoulder to ride on. Instead, when sharing the road where there is no separate bike lane or shoulder, your first responsibility is to yourself and your own safety. Your best bet is to ride in the lane's right wheel track so that you have 2 to 4 feet of space from the edge of the road. This makes you more visible to drivers, who typically will be looking for other vehicles in that area of the road. Plus, in this location you are less likely to blend in with the rocks along a hairpin turn or the foliage of an open space area. Another trick is to add a little extra motion to your riding style. Occasionally shake your head, wiggle your handlebar, or even exaggerate your body motion while standing up out of the saddle. This helps you register in a driver's peripheral vision as well as helping to indicate your direction of travel.

Light up: Outfit yourself and your bike so that you are easy to see. Bright-colored clothing is always a good idea, especially items such as shoe covers and gloves, which can catch a driver's attention because they are often in motion. Your helmet is another potential eye-catcher. Add some reflective tape in the rear or even affix a small blinky light. Indeed, lights in front and rear are essential, especially at dawn and dusk or whenever daylight is low.

Follow the flow: When riding in a standard road lane, ride on the right, but not too far right. Yes, this puts you closer to the flow of traffic, but it's also safer because drivers will be less tempted to try to squeeze past you. Not hugging the gutter also reduces your risk of getting walloped when someone opens the door of a parked car. Claim the entire lane, if that's what you need to ensure safety. In fact, on some streets that feature special lane markings (known as sharrows) cyclists are supposed to take the entire lane. Taking the full lane is often the safest way to ride downhill sections where the speed limit is 30 miles per hour or less, because a bike can easily keep up with other vehicles. In this case it's better to just act like a car.

Stay in your lane: Even if there is space, don't move to the right at intersections or when a long string of parking spaces is empty just to momentarily get out of the flow of traffic. You will have to move back into traffic at some point, perhaps popping out unexpectedly into a driver's view. Instead, hold your position and try to be as predictable as possible.

Take up your position: Use your position within the lane to signal your intentions. If you are preparing to merge or turn left, move to the left part of the lane. Stay in the center when you are traveling straight and moving at the same speed as other traffic. Move right when you want to merge or turn in that direction, or to permit cars to pass.

Eye oncoming traffic: Always keep an eye out for cars coming from the opposite direction that are about to make a left turn (across your path). This often happens when you trail a string of cars through an intersection. The driver coming the other way may be looking out only for cars, and he could start turning after the last car comes through the intersection because he's not expecting one more set of wheels to come through. To help avoid this

Chart Your Course

Take a page from the world of car and motorcycle safety and utilize the SIPDE method, which stands for: scan, identify, predict, decide, execute. Here's a breakdown of each.

➤ Scan the street (and sidewalk) ahead

➤ Identify potential hazards

➤ Predict their movements

➤ Decide on a course of action

➤ Execute the maneuver that takes you safely along your chosen line

Continuously split your attention among your immediate line through traffic, your escape route (an alternate line in case your path is blocked), side streets, and any traffic you have passed that might overtake you later. Don't get distracted by any vehicles, sounds, or events outside your line. Just note them and decide if they will enter your line later.

situation, try to stick close to the last car in the line. And of course be pre-pared to hit the brakes just in case.

Avoid getting squeezed: Drivers may sometimes try to sneak past you then cut you off when they turn right. One clue to watch for is when a car drifts toward the left side of the lane as it approaches the intersection, setting up for the quick turn to the right. Again, it's critical that you continuously scan and be ready to brake. For this reason, don't hug the side of road. This only encourages aggressive drivers to try to pass from behind when it's not safe.

Watch for blind spots: Drivers look for openings in traffic by nosing their cars out of driveways and side streets that have limited visibility. When you approach such spots, stand tall on the pedals and try to make eye contact with the driver. Take the center of the lane if you can, and check for escape space to the left just in case.

Chapter 12

STREET SMARTS

In addition to mastering the basic skills discussed in the last chapter, it's important for you to have a certain amount of street smarts when heading out into urban traffic. Heed these tips and tricks and you'll improve your chances of having a safe and drama-free bicycle commute.

Be prepared: Whenever you stop, be ready for an emergency takeoff. Keep your foot on the high pedal while you check behind. If that bus driver coming up from the rear happens to not notice you, you will want to be able to move and move fast.

Gear up: Riding in the city introduces a new set of obstacles to overcome. To reduce the chance of a flat tire, consider running slightly beefier tires with more puncture protection. There are many commuter and training-specific tires on the market that offer such features as bead-to-bead protection, Kevlar belts, increased tread life, and wet weather grip.

Also consider investing in a bell, lock, fenders, and rack. The bell is your bike's version of a horn, allowing you to alert pedestrians and other cyclists that you're approaching. The lock will help protect your valuable mode of transportation from bike thieves. Fenders will keep road spray at bay. Racks are great to have if you plan on carrying anything more than a shoulder bag.

Other handy items include a bandanna for wiping your face, hands, and bike. Have one for every day of the week, and a shower cap for covering your saddle when you park your bike outdoors in the rain. At the very least you should carry the essentials required to fix a flat tire, which include a spare tube, pump or CO_2 inflator, a pair of tire levers, and multitool.

If you have any doubts in your ability to use these items, see if your local bike shop offers a basic maintenance class, or search the Internet for how-to videos. The side of the road far from home is no place to discover you actually don't know how to change a tire on your own.

Timing is everything: Learn the rhythms of traffic in your city. For example, "the pulse" is a term that describes a series of timed traffic signals that create a mass of vehicles synchronized to catch green lights. Some riders may feel exhilarated riding with a wave of cars. If that's not your thing, look for routes on quieter streets, ideally with bike lanes. It's also possible to ride a timed street between the pulses, pulling over to let the mob of cars pass, then pedaling along in the empty spaces.

Find the best route: Even in your car, the freeway is not always the best way to get around. Over the years you've probably found some shortcuts to avoid high traffic areas during rush hour. These alternative routes are likely good candidates for your bike commute. It's also worth asking friends, other cyclists, and doing some research on the Internet in a quest to find more routes. Also check with your local parks or transportation department to see if they produce a map that features bike routes and multiuse paths.

Another strategy is to head out on your bike over the weekend and explore. Traffic patterns will differ some, but you can still find out which roads have bike lanes or ample shoulders, and which are not cyclist friendly. Be on the lookout for side streets, bike paths, and trails that can work into your route. If you have friends who commute, find out which routes they use. Even if they don't start their ride from the same neighborhood as you, they may be able to provide advice on areas that are closer to your destination.

No matter which route you choose, remember that cyclists bear the same responsibilities as drivers. Obey traffic laws, use hand signals to make others aware of your intentions, and always ride with the flow of traffic, not against it or on sidewalks. And, of course, always wear a helmet. It could save your life.

Steer smart: At speeds above 5 miles per hour, countersteering is the ideal way to execute a quick, evasive swoop around a road hazard or to curve inside a car's turning radius when you're cut off at a corner. This technique makes even a clunker agile because it uses the bike's own weight and wheels to rapidly initiate the turn. (For a full detailing of this technique, check out Chapter 8.)

When executing a countersteer maneuver, just make sure to be aware of your own lean angle. Many cyclists lean their bikes and not their bodies, which widens your turning radius and lessens the countersteer. Also make sure that you don't weave into traffic when you countersteer. Better to hit a pothole than broadside a Pontiac.

Bunnyhop obstacles: If you can't avoid road hazards such as potholes, ride over them as lightly as possible. More experienced riders can usually bunnyhop an obstacle. This is done by pressing down on the handlebar to compress the front tire, then lifting up on the bar and curling it forward while pulling up on the pedals to bring up the rear wheel.

Practice this technique on a grassy field or empty parking lot before trying it on a busy street. First, level your pedals as you approach the obstacle. Just before impact, lift the front of the bike, or at least take your weight off it. When the front wheel clears the obstacle, lean forward to take your weight off the rear wheel and pedal away. Use this same technique for hopping up a curb head-on.

To safely go from the curb back to the street, reverse the process. Level your pedals. Lean back on the seat as your front wheel drops over the curb. Then, lean onto the bar when the front wheel touches down. If the curb is high, hop lightly off the pedals as the back of the bike drops down to street level. Be sure that clearing a curb doesn't distract you from other obstacles around you.

Respect pedestrians: One reality of city riding is that you will occasionally end up on the sidewalk. First off, know that riding a bike on the sidewalk is illegal in some cities and may incur a ticket. And even if it's not against traffic laws, remember that this is not your place and you are a guest. When passing pedestrians, make sure to give plenty of notice by ringing your bell, whistling, or shouting to alert them of your presence. Do this no less than 10 feet away so that they have time to move and are less likely to be scared or startled.

Take your place: When approaching a red traffic light or stop sign, take

Make a Difference

To help make the streets safer for all cyclists, join and support a local, state, or national advocacy organization. Also try to find a way to volunteer or get involved, especially when it comes to local government decisions that impact whether roads are built strictly for cars, or if bicycles are considered, too. "Just a few people getting involved with city council can make a huge difference," says Scott Christopher of the cycling advocacy organization Bicycle Colorado. "In many cases, local elected officials don't hear from many of the citizens they represent, so your voice can make a difference."

your place in the line of traffic. Don't sneak up the right side and cut the line. This may force a motorist who already safely passed you to do it again. When you behave on your bike just as you do when driving a car, it will help ingratiate you with drivers who may otherwise not be enthusiastic about sharing the road with cyclists.

Leave early: Make sure to leave early enough for work that you have plenty of time to get to the workplace safely and get cleaned up and changed before the work day gets rolling.

Find partners: See if you can convince a few coworkers to join you. Riding with friends is fun, and cars are more likely to see a group of riders.

Keep a log: Track your miles ridden and you'll see just how much you saved in gas, and how many calories you've burned.

CARGO CARRYING OPTIONS

Unless you want to spend your entire workday in your cycling clothes, you will need to figure out how to get a change of clothes to your workplace. If you plan on riding to work every day, consider bringing in clothes for the week on the Friday before. That way you'll have everything you need when you get to work.

Also remember that in addition to your work attire, always carry a pump or CO_2 inflator, spare tube, a set of tire levers, and a multitool. To make sure you're prepared, consider laying everything out the night before, so you don't have to spend valuable morning time getting things together. If your commute is particularly long, pack a snack so you don't bonk. And if you don't have extra storage space at work, you are going to need a way to carry things on your bike. Here are some options.

Panniers: These are often the best cargo carrying option because they mount on your bike. Using panniers means you won't be restricted to how much you can carry on your back and still comfortably ride. Panniers also lower your center of gravity, providing a more stable ride. To install them, you'll need a rack and compatible bike frame.

Racks: These are a great option if you don't have much to carry, or if your commute is short enough that you can ride in your work clothes. Racks are the perfect size for carrying a bag of toiletries and a pair of shoes. You can also combine them with panniers to increase cargo-carrying capacity. Just make sure you bike has rack mounts before buying one.

Backpack: Depending on your pack's size, it should provide you with plenty of room to carry a change of clothes, toiletries, and your lunch. If your commute is long, make sure your backpack provides plenty of support by way of a chest strap and waist belt.

Messenger bag: These versatile bags are built for on-the-bike cargo carrying. Most have ample room for clothes, shoes, a lunch, and even a laptop. And the single shoulder-strap design makes it easy to dig out items without taking the bag off, such as when fishing out your wallet while making a coffee stop along the way.

Chapter 13

RIDING AT NIGHT

Though it may sound intimidating at first, there's something quite thrilling about riding a bike at night. Even familiar roads become new again when you're gliding along in your bubble of light. The air is cooler, and because visibility is limited, you seem to hear more. The stars form a magical canopy. On a quiet moonlit back road you can even switch off your headlight to fully enjoy the ivory aura.

Indeed, lots of cyclists ride at night, most of the time during their commute to and from work. Apprehension is a normal initial feeling, but typically that fear usually gives way to a feeling of fun. Modern cycling-specific headlights light up the road, while high-powered taillights and reflective clothing alert drivers that there is a cyclist ahead.

Alas, it is also true that many car/bike accidents happen at night. And that's why it pays to understand the equipment and techniques that can help you reduce the chances of calamity.

See and be seen: Even if you ride where there are streetlights bright enough to show you the way, it is still always best to ride with a headlight mounted on the front of your bike. In fact, it's the law in many states. And even when a headlight is not mandatory, having one still helps motorists and pedestrians see you.

Types of headlights run a wide gamut. Some cost hundreds of dollars and are nearly as bright as those on your car. Others are more affordable and primarily serve as a means to be seen rather than actually see. Consider your own typical circumstances when deciding what type of light you need.

Small battery-powered lights are usually reasonably priced and produce an adequate beam, making them a good choice for riding under streetlights or for short distances in the dark.

Cyclists who regularly ride at night usually invest in rechargeable models with multiple brightness settings. These brighter lights enhance safety and can inspire confidence. Battery life for most models ranges from 1 to 4 hours per charge, depending on how much you use the highest beam setting. If you don't need the light to see, you can extend battery life by using a burst or flash setting, which still does a good job of alerting motorists of your presence on the street.

Whether or not your state requires a taillight, it is still advisable to use one. There are lots of relatively inexpensive battery-powered models from which to choose. Most have light-emitting diodes (LEDs), which are typically more durable and brighter than standard bulbs. That's why most emergency transport vehicles use LED taillights.

Also consider adding reflective accents to the mix. Apply reflective tape to your frame, wheel rims (though not on the braking surfaces, of course), shoes, and/or helmet. In addition, wear cycling apparel that's specifically designed for riding at night; it will utilize bright colors and accents to help keep you more visible in low light conditions.

Riding techniques: Traffic laws don't change at night, but the general rules for safe cycling

Today's bike lights offer bright beams and long run times in a small package.

do. Vehicles (bikes included) are most easily identified by the light they emit or reflect. This is another reason that it pays to go overboard with lights and reflective material. The quicker a driver notices you and identifies that you are a cyclist, the less chance there is of an accident.

One potential danger is outriding your headlight. That is, going too fast to react quickly enough should something dangerous enter your beam. This is less likely to happen if you have one of the premium rechargeable light systems. Generally speaking, it's best to resist the temptation to go really fast during a night ride, unless Russian roulette is your idea of an acceptable risk.

Wet roads also reduce the distance that you can see well. Your headlight beam glances off the shiny, smooth surface and diffuses, leaving the road darker and less defined than when it's dry. Combine this reduced visibility with the increased time it takes for brakes to work when wet, and the danger doubles. Just as you would do if driving a car, adjust your riding speed to match the road conditions.

Try not to ever look directly into the lights of an oncoming car. Instead, hone your gaze on the right edge of the road so that you can avoid being blinded. This practice will also help you maintain a straight line. Some riders use a visor on their helmet so they can tip their head to block oncoming headlights.

Above all, ride defensively. Doing this is always a good idea, but after dark be even more cautious, especially at intersections. In the mix of movement and lights, always assume that drivers do not see you even when you have the right of way. Then, when you are safely away from congestion, relax and enjoy being on your bike at night.

Chapter 14

DEALING WITH INTERSECTIONS

Intersections are where all of your traffic riding skills come together. If you can ride through intersections smoothly and confidently, you should be able to handle almost any commuter-related cycling situation.

The basics are simple. Move to the correct lane position depending on which way you want to go (right, left, or straight ahead). This may mean leaving your normal position near the right side of the road. If you're turning right, keep to the right. If you're turning left, move to the center of the road. If you're going straight, set up between the right- and left-turning traffic.

Turning right: Right turns are easiest. Just stay in the right lane, check for traffic, signal your intention by extending your right arm, and go around the corner. To avoid being squeezed against the curb of a narrow road by a car trying to pass, ride in the middle of the right lane. Also remember that the rear of a car moves to the right as it makes a right turn.

At a stop sign or a traffic light where you can legally turn right on red, yield to through traffic coming from the left and to pedestrians on crosswalks. Always remember that cyclists are obligated to follow the same rules as drivers.

Look back, look ahead: You will need to change lane position for some intersection maneuvers. In fact, for some left turns you must move across more than one lane. This technique begins with looking back to check for traffic. Because your sense of balance is in your head, you should practice turning your head without swerving.

Some riders change lane position without looking back because they're afraid of swerving. Bad idea. Don't trust your ears. In this age of electric and hybrid cars, many motorized vehicles are very quiet. Plus, you need to watch out for other cyclists, too. Even if you use a rearview mirror, you should still glance back. A mirror will reveal traffic that is directly behind you but will not alert you to any vehicles at your side.

Now that you have checked behind, you'll need to make some quick decisions. If there is a car close, let it pass and deal with the next one. The later driver will have time to react to your signals. If you make your intentions clear, you will almost always be permitted to move into the lane. Extend your left arm to signal your wish to move left. Wait a couple of seconds, then look back again to check that the driver has slowed down or has moved aside to make room for you.

Turning your head to look back is a signal, too. In slow, crowded traffic you need to keep your hands on the handlebar, ready to brake. You can usually move into line with the cars after signaling with a turn of your head. Make sure that the driver has made room for you. Most will, but there is no guarantee. If possible, try to make eye contact with the driver. It is not your signal that makes it safe to change lanes. It is the driver's acceptance of your signal and her appropriate reaction to your presence that gives you safe passage.

If you begin your lane change early enough to deal with two drivers, you will almost always succeed. If the first one doesn't make room, the second one almost certainly will. In a high-speed traffic situation, though, drivers may not have time to react. Then you need to wait for a gap big enough to allow you to move safely across all lanes at once.

Turning left: To prepare for a left turn, change lanes until you reach the road's left-turn position. This is where all of the cars on your left will also turn left and none will go straight. If the lane carrying left-turning traffic also carries through traffic, ride at its left side. If it's a left-turn-only lane, ride at its right side. On an ordinary two-lane street, set up just to the right of the center line.

It may seem dangerous to move to the middle of the street, but this is the best position for a left turn. It puts all the traffic you have to deal with in front of you. Because you're to the left of the through traffic coming from

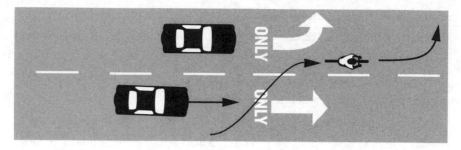

If the lane carrying left-turning vehicles also carries through traffic, ride at its left side. If it's a left-turn-only lane, ride at its right side as pictured here.

behind, you don't have to look back before turning left. Instead you can fully focus on the traffic from the left, right, and front.

If you have to cross more than one lane to reach the left turn position, do it in steps. First, cross the lane line so that you are just inside the next lane. Second, cross to the far side of the lane. At each step look back and signal drivers to make room for you.

Yield to traffic entering the intersection. You can roll slowly forward, the way cars do, so that you can move fast when there is a gap in the traffic. Pass an oncoming left-turning vehicle right side to right side.

When turning left from the left side of a lane, do not let left-turning cars behind you pass on your right. While waiting, make a "slow" signal with your right hand (arm extended downward, open hand facing to the rear). Ride straight ahead for a few feet as you enter the intersection, allowing left turning cars behind you to pass on your left.

It is also okay to hop off your bike at the right side of the road, then make a left turn as a pedestrian. This way you can turn left legally at a "no left turn" sign or avoid dangerous traffic situations that are beyond your comfort zone.

Stay straight: It is usually easy to ride straight through an intersection. You may have to change lanes, but not many. The key is to make sure that right-turning traffic passes you on your right. Stay completely out of the right-turn-only lane. If there is a lane marked for right turns and through traffic, ride near its left side. On a multilane road, you may have to move into the second or third lane from the curb to avoid right-turning traffic.

The most difficult intersection to ride straight through is a small two-lane street. This is because traffic in the right lane could go in any of three directions: right, left, or straight. On a street with parallel parking, the empty space between the last parked car and the corner serves as a right-turn lane. Don't wander into this space. Stay in the traffic lane.

On a street without parking, pull a little farther into the lane to discourage right-turning drivers from passing you on the left and then cutting you off. When stopping at a light, it is considerate to position yourself far enough from the curb so that drivers can turn right on red. If they hesitate to roll through, wave them by with your right hand.

Chapter 15

EVASIVE MANEUVERS

The bicycle is a highly maneuverable tool, which is both good and bad. It's good because as your riding skills improve, that maneuverability will help you avoid obstacles and dangerous situations. But it is bad because one small mistake can result in a crash. As you have surely noticed by now, bikes tip over pretty easily.

Here are six basic techniques that every road cyclist should have in their repertoire of skills. When you master these emergency maneuvers, you'll become a more confident, relaxed, and safe bike rider.

Avoiding obstacles: Thanks to your bike's maneuverability, you can learn to handle challenging situations. For example, say that you are rolling down a pleasant two-lane country road, just wide enough for cars to pass you in your lane. You look up at the scenery and then down at the road. Watch out! There's a rock dead ahead. You also hear a car just behind. So you know you can't swerve left into traffic, and you don't want to swerve right onto gravel. So what to do?

Enter the "rock dodge" maneuver, which allows your wheels to weave

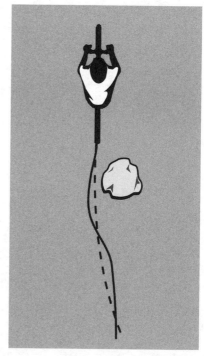

There are two choices in this situation: dodge the rock or bunny hop it.

around the rock while continuing to ride in a straight line. Here's how it is done. Just as you reach the rock, quickly steer left, then right to correct your balance, then straight again. Because you correct your balance quickly, your body doesn't have time to follow the bike's weave. You continue in a nearly straight line as you safely navigate around the hazard. To master the rock dodge, go to an empty parking lot and practice until it becomes easy.

Turning quickly: Picture yourself in another dicey situation. This time you are riding down the street toward an intersection. A car on your left suddenly begins a right turn and you're headed straight toward the car's side. To avoid hitting the car, you need to execute a sharp turn. But how?

Your bicycle balances the same way you balance a stick on the palm of your hand. If you want to quickly move the stick to the right, you move your hand to the left. Then the stick leans to the right, and you follow it with your hand. Similarly, if you twitch your bike out from under you by steering to the left for an instant, you can then turn sharply to the right. The hard part is making yourself steer momentarily toward the car you are trying to avoid.

Practice this technique in your favorite parking lot. Going slowly at first, snap the handlebar quickly to the left. Your bike will lean to the right, and then you can steer right. As you get the hang of it, increase your speed. The faster you go, the less sharply you have to steer.

This "instant turn" technique is useful in many situations. If a car coming toward you begins a dangerous left turn, turn right onto the side street with it. If a car emerges from a side street on the right, turn onto the side street. It's best to turn to the right, behind the car. But if it's too late, turn left with the car. Even if you hit it, the closer you are to parallel, the lighter the impact will be.

Handling curves: At some point in your cycling career, you will find yourself going around a downhill curve too fast. Without evasive action, you may end up in the crosshairs of oncoming traffic—or crashing into a ditch on the other side of the road. To avoid calamity, use a variation of the instant turn to get you through this situation in one piece.

The usual panic reaction in this situation is to slam on the brakes. But doing this will only serve to straighten the bike and may send you headfirst off the road before you can stop. Instead, steer with the curve, and (maybe) feather your brakes. Straighten the handlebar momentarily, as in an instant turn, to drop your bike into a deeper lean. Stand hard on the outside pedal. You'll be surprised how far you can angle your wheels without losing traction. But if you do slide out and go down, you'll only skid on your side and come to a stop. That's much better than sailing across the road and perhaps hitting an oncoming car or guardrail head-on.

If you're about to ride into a wall or off the edge of the road, it may be better to deliberately slide down. Lean into the turn then hit the brakes. The fall will hurt, but probably not as much as the alternative.

Hopping over hazards: This time there's a pothole straight ahead, but you don't have enough time to execute a rock dodge maneuver. Time to bunny-hop! This is the quickest last-resort way to avoid a pothole or another road-surface hazard. Once you get good at it, you can even jump over low curbs or railroad tracks. See Chapter 12 for instructions.

Ignore angry drivers: As tempting as it may be, if a driver buzzes by you, yells out the window, or otherwise wrongs you, resist the urge to reply with a middle-finger salute. Instead, take a deep breath and remember

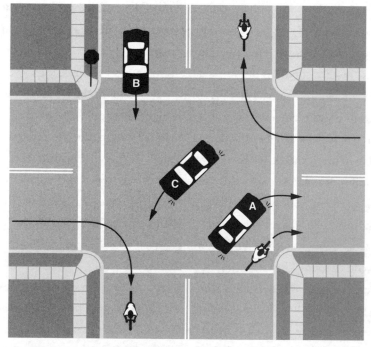

The "instant turn" can help you escape a number of dicey situations.

that your main priority is to get where you are going safely. Indeed, the natural fight-or-flight response can often lead to escalation of an already bad situation. And, when in doubt, remember the old law enforcement joke that says any confrontation on the road will be won by the combatant with the most lug nuts, and you don't have any.

Accident protocol: If you are involved in an accident, draw upon your experience from operating a car, advises Scott Christopher of the cycling advocacy organization Bicycle Colorado. "Ask yourself, what do you think your insurance company would want you to do," says Christopher. "Don't rush. Think legally. Don't take blame, and include law enforcement in the process, asking the police officer for a complete accident report. Bottom line is that it is two vehicles that have gotten into an accident, so it should be treated the same way as a standard car-on-car accident would. That's also another reason why you need to obey the same traffic rules as cars. If you roll a stop sign and then get hit, it's probably your fault."

Chapter 16

CRITICAL SURVIVAL SKILLS

No matter how skilled or prepared you are, some cycling situations will go beyond the normal rules. Here are some critical tips and tricks for dealing with three unique situations faced by cyclists in the city.

Traffic congestion: Getting caught in a traffic jam doesn't have to mean standing in the road breathing auto exhaust. Indeed, avoiding this is one of the biggest advantages of riding a bike in a city. Just make sure to take extra caution when negotiating in close quarters with cars. Stopped cars in a traffic jam present many of the same hazards as parked cars: blind spots, opening doors, and unpredictable starts, stops, and turns.

If there is an open passing lane, use it rather than threading between cars. If the street is completely plugged, slowly pick your way forward with your hands on the brake levers. Remember, any car door could suddenly open.

In a total jam, you can be fairly sure that cars won't move, because they have nowhere to go. But if there is an open driveway or a parking space into which a car could turn, you have to assume that a car will go for it. Look to see whether a car's front wheels are turned. Move away from the side of the car as you pass. Try to get the driver's attention and make eye contact as you approach the front of the car.

When cars are stopped but not completely bumper to bumper, watch out for drivers from other lanes trying to dart into the gaps. Stop and look before you move into a gap yourself.

Don't pass a long truck or bus stuck in a traffic jam unless there's an open lane next to it. As you ride close to the side of such a vehicle, it may begin to merge in your direction, leaving you no way to escape.

When you approach an intersection, change lanes to take the same position that you would in normal traffic. Before you cross in front of a car, you'll again want to make eye contact with the driver, even if the car is stopped. When you reach the intersection, wait behind the first car at a red traffic light. Don't move up next to it. Drivers don't always use turn signals, so you can't be sure which way the car might turn when the light turns green.

Sidewalks and bicycle paths: Many people assume that sidewalks are safe to ride on because they put some distance between cyclists and cars. In reality, sidewalks are not a good place to ride your bike, and in some cities it's actually illegal. Try to avoid them unless you have no choice.

Trees, hedges, parked cars, buildings, and doorways create blind spots along sidewalks, which are typically too narrow to allow you enough operating space to swerve out of the way if someone or something crosses your path. A pedestrian can sidestep suddenly, or a small child can run out from behind an adult. That's why you should never pass a pedestrian until you first have their attention. Also remember that cars use sidewalks at every driveway. Thus you need to ride slowly and look in all directions before crossing anyplace a car may appear.

Multiuse paths can have these same problems. Even if bicycles are supposed to have the right of way, the path may be too narrow for safe maneuvering. And, again, pedestrians are often unpredictable and intersections are often hazardous. A bike path can get crowded with skaters, joggers, dog walkers, and careless, inexperienced riders.

Remember, you don't have to use a bike path just because it's there. It may provide a useful shortcut, and it may be pleasant and scenic, but sometimes a street with a bike lane will provide a better route for competent cyclists. Realize, though, that if you ride on a road that has a parallel bike path, some drivers may become upset. Some drivers believe that you should use a bike path if it's available. As they rush by, there is no way you can explain that the path is narrow and hazardous. You may be able to avoid this problem by choosing a different route.

Large vehicles: From your bike you can see over most cars. But don't let this vantage point lull you into a false sense of security. You can't see over a large van, a truck, or a bus. Moving blind spots lurk behind these tall vehicles, and that means increased danger for you.

Suppose you are riding on a two-way, four-lane street. You have merged to the inside lane because you want to turn left. You signal and continue to move forward. You see only one other vehicle on the street: a van, coming toward you in the opposite passing lane. It stops to let you turn left. Can you safely make your turn?

No. Because you are moving forward, a blind spot behind the van is, in effect, moving toward you. If a car is passing the van in the outside lane, you won't see it. If you turn, you could have a terrible accident. That means you need to be more patient and cautious around larger vehicles, always waiting to make your move until after you have a clear view and can confirm that it's safe to proceed.

Earn respect: There will always be people in cars who yell, "Get off the road!" Don't let them bother you. Ride in ways that encourage drivers to maneuver around you correctly. Signal clearly. Be a good representative of cycling and a positive role model for riders in your community. When more cyclists do it right, drivers will have an easier time and become friendlier.

In the long run, drivers will understand that it makes sense to share the road. Bicycles take up less space than cars, are environmentally friendly, and every person who chooses to ride a bike is reducing traffic congestion. Every day, by your presence on the road, you are helping to establish the benefits of cycling.

Part Four
ESSENTIAL BICYCLE MAINTENANCE

Chapter 17

BASIC PRE-RIDE CHECKUP

It's Friday night. You have a 100-mile gran fondo on tap the next day. You're fueled up, hydrated, and all your essential gear and apparel is laid out and ready to go. But what about your bike? It's always a good idea to give your two-wheeled machine a quick once-over before a major race or ride. It will increase the likelihood that you catch small problems that could lead to a mechanical breakdown or accident during your big event.

A routine tune-up typically takes about an hour. As long as you have the right tools, it's a manageable task for even a B-grade home mechanic. Besides addressing potential problems, it will boost your confidence that you can handle anything that might happen out on the road.

Keep in mind that the procedure outlined in this chapter is only applicable to a reasonably maintained bike that's in good working condition. If your rig has been collecting dust in the back of your garage for several years, have a professional mechanic give it a thorough tune-up.

Here are the key tools you'll need, plus a step-by-step guide for performing a basic bike checkup.

➤ Allen wrench set

➤ Brake pads (if necessary)

➤ Bucket

➤ Chain lube

➤ Degreaser

➤ Detergent

➤ Pump

➤ Rags

➤ Repair stand

➤ Spoke wrench

➤ Sponge

➤ Tires (if necessary)

A clean bike is a happy bike, and that includes the chain.

Step 1. Place your bike in a repair stand. If the bike is only slightly dirty, just give it a good wipe down with a rag. If it is truly dirty, remove both wheels and wash thoroughly. If the drivetrain is really grimy, spray the chain and derailleurs with degreaser and let the bike sit for a few minutes. Fill the bucket with warm, soapy water. Wet a sponge, hold it on the chain, and turn the crank to draw the chain through the sponge until the links are clean. Clean the crankset and derailleurs as well. Then clean the frame and parts (including the wheels) with a fresh sponge. Rinse by dripping water from above. (Don't spray directly at the bike because this can force water into the bearings.) Dry the bike and all parts with rags.

Step 2. Stand in front of the bike, holding the fork in one hand and the down tube in the other. Push and pull on the fork to check for play in the headset. Rotate the fork slowly from side to side to feel for roughness. If it's loose or tight, loosen the stem binder bolts, then remove play or tightness by adjusting the Allen screw atop the stem, and finish by securing the stem bolts. Now check the bottom bracket bearings. Stand beside the frame, hold the crank arms, and push and pull, feeling for play. Most bottom brackets are sealed and reliable. If yours is loose, have a shop remove the crank arms and adjust it.

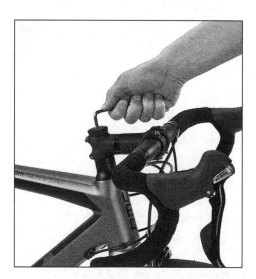

Make sure there is no play in your headset by properly tightening the stem cap.

Step 3. Inspect the tires for cracks, cuts, blisters, and baldness. Replace tires, as needed. Also, check tire seating. There are lines on the base of the sidewalls that should sit just above the rim all the way around. If they dip below the rim edge or rise above it, the tire is not seated properly. If you find any of these problems, deflate the tire and reinflate it, making sure that it seats correctly. Reinstall the wheels on the bike, making sure that they are centered in the frame and the quick-releases are properly tightened.

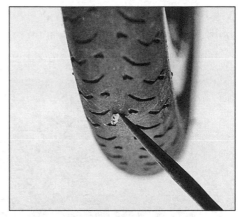

If you spot a piece of debris lodged in your tire, try carefully picking it out.

Step 4. Starting at the valve stem, work your way around each wheel, wiggling the spokes to see if any are loose. After checking a few spokes, you'll get a feel for the correct tension. If you find loose spokes, tighten them by turning the nipple clockwise with a spoke wrench (when sighted from above) in half-turn increments. Then spin the wheels and sight trueness by looking at the gap between the rim and brake pad. If you see a wobble, you'll need to true the wheel. This is a more complex process and is best left to a bike shop mechanic unless you are an experienced home mechanic. As a primer on truing, to move the rim to the left, loosen right-side nipples and tighten left-side nipples in the problem area. Do the reverse to move it right. Always turn nipples a half-turn at a time and check progress. Patience is key here.

Tighten loose spokes by turning the nipple clockwise.

Step 5. Though major components should not come loose during normal use, it is still wise to check them periodically. Without forcing, tighten crank bolts, pedals, chainring bolts, stem binder, handlebar binder, seat binder, seat bolt, brake and derailleur attaching nuts/bolts, and bottle cage screws.

It's a good idea to check and snug chainring bolts from time to time.

(Everything is turned clockwise to tighten except the left pedal, which is turned counterclockwise.) Also, make sure all your repair gear is in proper working order, including pump or CO_2 inflator. Finally, put a drop of lube on the pivot points of clipless pedals, derailleurs, and brakes.

Step 6. If they are not internally routed, lube shift cables where they pass under the bottom bracket. Lube the chain, then shift through the gears repeatedly to test derailleur adjustments. Because the rear derailleur's cable is longer and gets more use, it's more likely to go out of adjustment. Each click of the rear shift lever should cause the chain to immediately

Keeping your chain properly lubricated is critical to a properly functioning (not to mention quiet) bike.

jump to the next cog. If not, the cable has probably stretched slightly, or you may have mistakenly adjusted it too tightly. If the chain hesitates to go to a larger cog, the cable is slightly loose. If the chain is slow in moving to a smaller cog, the cable is too tight. Fix slow shifts to larger cogs by turning the adjustment barrel on the rear of the derailleur counterclockwise in half-turn increments. For slow shifts to smaller cogs, do the opposite.

For electronic shifting systems, do the same test, running through both front and rear shifting to make sure everything is operating properly. If you do discover any problems, consult the appropriate troubleshooting manual for your components (Shimano, SRAM, or Campagnolo) to help diagnose and remedy the problem. Adjusting electronic systems is typically much easier than traditional mechanical shifting drivetrains. In fact, as long as your battery is adequately charged, it's unlikely you'll have to do much adjusting at all. Just make sure you're fully charged before the big ride. Without a charged battery, your electronic system will not work. There's nothing worse than being stuck in one gear all day.

Step 7. Inspect all four brake pads. If the grooves are worn away, it is time to replace the pads. Make sure that they strike the rim squarely. If not, use an Allen wrench to loosen the nut that secures the pad and reposition it. Squeeze the brake levers to feel the action. The pads should strike the rim well before the levers approach the handlebar. If not, tighten the brake by turning the barrels on the brake calipers. If it's one piece, turn it counterclockwise until the pads are $^1/_8$ to $^1/_4$ inch away from the rim.

If your bike is equipped with

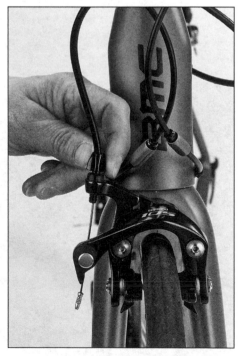

A small turn of your brake's barrel adjuster will move your pads in or out.

disc brakes, you'll need to remove the wheels to inspect the pads. Once the wheels are off, assure that your pads have at least 1.5mm of braking material left. Anything less and it's time for a new set of brake pads. Also make sure that your braking system is working properly by squeezing the levers several times while the wheel and rotor are in place. If the lever action feels mushy or the lever pulls all the way to the bars before engaging, it's likely time for a brake bleed. This is another advanced-level maintenance task, so if you're not an experienced mechanic, take your bike to the shop and get the brakes checked and bled if necessary.

Step 8. Once you've run through all these steps, take your bike for a short test ride. Shift and brake repeatedly, making adjustments as necessary. Now you are ready for your big ride, confident that as long as your body cooperates there is nothing to prevent you from successfully getting to the finish line.

Time permitting, take a short test spin before heading out for your all day affair.

Chapter 18
SPRING BIKE PREP

Ah, springtime, when days grow longer—and, more important, warmer—signaling the start of another glorious cycling season. And that means it is time to dust off your bike and get back on the road. But before you start turning the cranks, it is a good idea to give your bike a tip-to-tail once over. Whether you spent the winter splashing through ice and mud, sweating away on a trainer, or not riding at all, your bike could almost certainly benefit from TLC. Follow this step-by-step guide and you will be rolling again in no time.

A clean bike is a happy bike: Using a mild detergent and warm water, give your bike a bath. This will brighten its appearance and extend the overall lifespan of the frame and components by removing sweat and corrosive road spray. Once washing is done, lather some degreaser on the drivetrain to remove any remaining grit and grime. Then relubricate critical moving parts, especially the chain.

Tire check: Winter riding is tough on tires, especially if you use a trainer. Roller wheels can wear away the center of a tire quicker than normal use. If your tire looks worn or flattened on the center tread, mount up a new pair.

Replace cables and housing: If your bike is equipped with a mechanical shifting drivetrain and/or cable actuated brakes (rim or disc), you'll want to examine cables and housing. Just as with your drivetrain, corrosive sweat from trainer rides or grime from slushy winter roads can cause them to gunk up and not work properly. That is why spring is a great time to replace cables and housing. When installing new cable, coat it with a tiny bit of chain lube. This will further improve your bike's shifting and braking performance.

Tune it up: If you are not comfortable working on your bike, head down to your favorite local bike shop and get your bike tuned up. Just remember that springtime is often the busiest time of year for these stores, so it's best to call ahead and make a reservation.

Saddlebag check: Whether your first ride of the year will be a casual spin around the block or an all-day epic into the high mountains, you need to carry the basic gear required to fix a flat tire. That means your jersey pocket or saddlebag must contain a spare tube, a pair of tire levers, a small hand

Measuring Chain Wear

Besides your tires, your bike's chain is arguably the component that needs the most frequent replacing. Wait too long, and your chain will wear out, diminishing shifting quality and shortening the lifespan of the rest of your drivetrain components.

So how often should you replace your chain? Before answering that question, it helps to understand the process of chain wear. As your chain ages, each link's internal bushings slowly lengthen. In turn, your now-longer chain puts added pressure on your cassette cogs and chainring teeth, causing them to wear faster. This also hampers shifting quality.

To avoid this accelerated wear of your cassette and chainrings, a general rule of thumb is to replace your bike's chain every 2,000 miles. This is just a starting point. No two chains will wear at exactly the same rate because no two riders treat their chains the same.

If you're the type who spins easy gears, meticulously cleans and lubes the chain after every ride, never rides in the rain, and weighs as much as a World Tour climbing specialist, your chain is likely to pump or CO_2 inflator, and a multitool. If you're not sure what's in there right now (or if it's still in working order), unload the bag and run through everything. You should do this before heading out on that first ride of the year—and repeat this checkup every month or so during the season.

Get a bike fit: If you swapped on new components during the offseason, such as a saddle, stem, pedals, or shoes, consider getting a professional bike fit. Even tiny changes can alter your on-bike efficiency and comfort.

last longer than 2,000 miles. But if you never miss a meal, love to push big gears, ride rain or shine all the time, and don't even own shop rags, getting 2,000 miles out of your chain is a pipedream.

These differences in riding style are why it is best to periodically use a chain wear measuring tool to determine the condition of your chain. With the tool in hand, apply pressure to a pedal so the top of the chain is taut, and then place the measuring tool in place and read the results. Indicators on the tool will tell you whether it's time to replace your chain.

You can also measure chain wear using a standard ruler. To do this, you should know that all modern chains have rivets every half-inch, and that you will be measuring from one rivet to another one that is 12 inches away.

Start by drawing the chain taut. Align the end of the ruler at the zero-inch mark with the center of a rivet, and then see where the ruler's 12 inch mark lines up. If it is dead center on a rivet, the chain is in great condition. If the rivet is less than a $\frac{1}{16}$ of an inch ahead of the 12 inch mark, then the chain is showing some wear but still has plenty of life left in it. If the rivet is more than $\frac{1}{16}$ of an inch ahead of the 12 inch mark, then it is time to replace your chain.

Part Five

TRAINING ON AND OFF THE BIKE

Chapter 19

BASIC BODY MECHANICS EXPLAINED

Your legs gradually awaken to the movement of another ride. The early moments of this 25-miler are difficult. But after a few minutes, your breathing increases in depth, your heart rate quickens, and you begin feeling fast and efficient, like a well-tuned cycling machine. Your body is deriving energy from the most abundant source, the air itself. You feel as though you could ride forever. But how far and how fast can you actually go?

There are three primary energy systems that you rely on as a cyclist: ATP–PC, glycolysis, and aerobic. By understanding these systems—and the fuel they burn—you can train in ways that make energy more abundant and reliable.

The process of using energy begins with adenosine triphosphate (ATP), which is the currency for energy exchange in the body. Muscles can't contract without it. ATP consists of an adenosine molecule linked to three phosphate molecules by high-energy chemical bonds. To liberate energy for muscular contraction, one of the phosphate molecules is released. You may not realize it as you ride, but this process is crucial. Your body's ability to satiate your muscles' need for ATP determines your performance.

Working muscles can get ATP from any of three primary energy systems (ATP–PC, glycolysis, and aerobic) depending on the situation. When you attack a hill, you need energy released quickly. A long, flat stretch, however, calls for steady production of ATP lasting many minutes or hours. Your body senses the difference and accordingly taps the appropriate system.

A limited amount of ATP exists in the muscle cell itself. It's found close to a moderately high energy compound called phosphocreatine (PC). This naturally occurring and immediately available ATP source is known as the ATP–PC or the adenosine triphosphate–phosphocreatine system. It's anaerobic, which means that it doesn't need oxygen to function. And though it's the most powerful energy supply in the body, it can be exhausted by 5 to 7 seconds of intense cycling. This is what sprinters tap into during the final fleeting moments of a race.

When this happens, the phosphocreatine splits into phosphate and creatine, creating fragments that can re-form into ATP. This extends the system's usefulness beyond those brief few seconds, but it still can't provide energy for more than 30 seconds. When you need a short burst of speed, this is the energy you use. After it's depleted, it's eventually replenished by ATP from other energy sources.

Another primary system is the glycolysis system, which isn't as powerful as the ATP–PC system, but the energy it provides lasts slightly longer. When you are grinding up a climb or unleashing an extended sprint, this is the energy source your body draws upon.

Glycolysis uses muscle glycogen (carbohydrate), then blood glucose, then, finally, liver glycogen as fuel to produce energy. These substances are broken down into ATP and lactic acid. This happens within your cells but not directly at the muscle contraction site. Because this process requires more than 10 chemical reactions, its rate of ATP production is slower than the ATP–PC system's. For up to 5 minutes, a large number of ATP molecules can be formed. Ultimately, excessive accumulation of lactic acid undermines this system by inhibiting muscular contraction. That burning sensation in your legs as you attack a steep hill is an example of the accumulation of lactic acid. Fortunately, you can train your body to delay the negative effects of lactic acid buildup through repeated hard efforts, such as interval training.

Last is your aerobic system. Of the three systems, only this one can provide energy almost indefinitely. Like the glycolysis system, it uses muscle glycogen, then blood glucose, then liver glycogen as fuel. It also taps slow-processing fat as an energy source.

What sets the aerobic system apart from the other systems is that it requires oxygen to produce ATP molecules. It also relies on multiple chemical reactions and a shuttle to move ATP from specialized production sites (called mitochondria) within the muscle cell to the contraction area. For these reasons the aerobic system is a slower producer of ATP, but it can produce the largest amount.

Intimately linked to the cardio-respiratory system, the aerobic system depends on a constant supply of oxygen molecules. These molecules are inhaled into the lungs for transfer to the blood, and are then delivered to the muscles by the heart. Training can improve delivery by enhancing the amount of blood pumped with each heartbeat, and can improve the ability of muscles to extract the oxygen when it arrives.

Generally, any effort longer than 5 minutes derives the majority of its energy from the aerobic system. A prolonged ride puts a cyclist in a so-called steady state, which means that the oxygen consumed for ATP production is equal to the ATP necessary for muscle contraction. Your ability to maintain a steady state depends on a combination of your genetic potential and your current fitness level.

The transition between anaerobic and steady-state cycling occurs early in a ride. Until a steady state is reached, the two anaerobic systems (ATP–PC and glycolysis) supply most of the ATP. So by starting out slow you can avoid unnecessarily reducing ATP or accumulating too much lactic acid. The more you train, the faster you can achieve the steady state. In just 2 minutes of riding, your aerobic system can become the predominant supplier of ATP.

SO WHAT DOES IT ALL MEAN ON THE BIKE?

When you do intervals—alternating intense hard efforts with easy ones—your breathing becomes labored and your muscles ache. Indeed, any extreme effort, such as a long sprint or climb, bathes muscles with lactic acid. Given time to recover, such as on a descent, the muscles partially clear themselves of waste so that they can be ready for the next hard burst. But they are never totally cleared on a given ride. The accumulation eventually allows lactic acid to cause fatigue and breathlessness.

At this point you can no longer rely on your first energy source. Phosphocreatine, having completed its short-term mission, is depleted. Your second energy source is paralyzed by its own by-product, lactic acid. Your body is then forced to use only oxygen to produce ATP, and the aerobic system can't provide energy as fast as your muscles need it.

The point at which lactic acid becomes debilitating is widely known as lactate threshold (LT). For competitive cyclists, normal race pace is just below LT, which allows them to use both aerobic and anaerobic energy. Thus, LT is a primary indicator of potential endurance performance.

LT tests are typically performed on a trainer at a sports science lab. After warming up, the test begins at an exercise intensity that corresponds to 50 to 60 percent of the test subject's oxygen consumption, or VO_2, max. Each stage lasts about 3 minutes, which allows enough time for the rider to achieve lactate production. At the end of each stage, blood samples are taken via finger prick, which reveals blood lactate. This process is repeated as the workload increases until an obvious spike in lactate concentration occurs. Heart rate and power are recorded at each stage, and the max numbers for each category become your threshold number, which can then be used in training when using a heart rate monitor or power meter.

If you don't have the wherewithal for lab testing, you can approximate lactate threshold and VO_2 max in the field using a power meter. After warming up for about 10 minutes, reset your device and capture data during an all-out, 30-minute effort. Now using training software such as Training Peaks or Strava, determine your average power for the final 20 minutes of the test. This number is an approximation of your lactate threshold (also known as functional threshold power or FTP). Next multiply that FTP number by 10.8, then divide by your weight in kilograms, and finally add seven. This is your VO_2 max. Men in their 20s average around 47. A number in the low 60s means you're an elite athlete. Above 70 is Olympic level.

Chapter 20

TIPS FOR GETTING FASTER

Now that you have a base understanding of what's going on inside your body when you're cycling, here are eight ways to increase the performance of your energy systems.

Go the distance: Your VO_2 max is largely determined by genetics, so improving it is not easy. High-intensity endurance work may raise your VO_2 max. One popular method for raising it is to ride just below lactate threshold (LT) for as long as possible. (Use a heart rate monitor or power meter to track this.) Begin by trying to maintain this intensity for 10 to 30 minutes. As your endurance increases, lengthen your workouts accordingly.

Ride hard, rest easy: Use interval training to increase your LT. This prevents lactic acid accumulation from disrupting high-intensity efforts. In fact, such training can increase the amount of creatine, phosphate, and ATP in your system and can enhance the use of some of the lactic acid.

Using a power meter or heart rate monitor as a guide, ride for 10 to 20 seconds at a pace that produces a pulse equal to 80 to 90 percent of your VO_2 max, then follow with a lower-intensity period of 1 to 3 minutes. As your LT rises, lengthen the work interval and shorten the recovery period. Be sure that you give yourself an easy or rest day after such intense training.

Build tolerance: Train with hill repeats and other hard efforts to teach your body to withstand increased amounts of lactic acid. This allows you to continue riding above your LT for longer periods, which is important for climbing and sprinting. One common workout is intervals lasting from 20 seconds to 3 minutes, interspersed with 30 to 60 seconds of recovery.

Keep the recovery interval short to make sure that the lactic acid level in your muscles stays high. Another method is to do longer 20- to 60-minute workouts at LT intensity with no recovery period.

Mix it up: One of the most common mistakes is riding at the same speed all the time. That's why so many coaches will tell you that their goal is to make

The Benefits of Having a Coach

If riding your bike is simply a hobby, something you do for entertainment and exercise, you probably don't need to hire a coach. Just keep riding and have fun doing it. But if at some point getting faster is a priority for you, then having a coach is your one-way ticket to increased speed. Perhaps you have decided to start racing. Or maybe you're targeting a century ride next summer. Whatever the case, a little guidance can go a long way toward helping you achieve your goals.

"For me, the biggest benefit of having a coach is that it forced me to be accountable," says Scott Moninger, former pro racer turned coach. "It's really beneficial to have someone telling you what to do in training. And with the advent of power meters, your coach can get a really good idea of what you're doing and where your fitness level is. As an athlete, I would rather just go do the work and have my coach worry about parsing the data."

A good coach will also be your number-one confidant, that person you can ask questions and bounce ideas off, says Jeremy Powers, multitime US national cyclocross champion.

"A lot of times it helps me see things from a different perspective," adds Powers. "Everyone will be different, but why not have an expert to explain to you how to do something rather than trying to figure it out all on your own, which can take a long time and will involve a lot of trial and error. Instead, that person can tell you when to ride, how much to ride, how hard to ride, what to eat, all the things that go along with becoming a better cyclists. Coaches are usually also good at pointing out and helping you work on your you ride harder than you ever have before—and easier than you've ever gone before. If you just ride your bike at the same medium-hard pace all the time, you'll just get tired.

Sleep: Strive for 7 to 9 hours of rest per night, especially during periods of intense training or racing.

weaknesses. And that can be hard to do on your own. It's human nature to just focus on what you are good at."

When it comes time to pick a coach, Frank Overton, owner and founder of FasCat Coaching in Boulder, Colorado, says to treat it like you're interviewing someone for a job.

"Ask questions about their philosophy, about their experience and credentials," he says. "Is coaching a career for them or just something they do on the side as a hobby because they think they can make an easy buck capitalizing on their personality or how fast they are."

Your prospective coach should also be readily able to provide testimonials or references from other athletes they've worked with. "If a coach can't do that, I would immediately start looking elsewhere," adds Overton.

The cost of coaching will vary greatly, but Overton says you should expect to pay somewhere between $150 and $300 a month for professional-grade services. Of course, you will also likely find someone willing to do it for $50, too. But the old adage of you get what you pay for applies. "That's the guy who probably has another job, and may or may not return your phone calls," warns Overton. "You don't want someone who is just copying and pasting training programs. You could do that yourself for free."

Finally, Overton recommends that you don't just hire a coach for a month or two. "Obviously I am a little biased, but you really need to give it 6 to 12 months to see the biggest benefits," he says. "The best results I see are usually with athletes that are in the second, third, or fourth year of getting coached and they never had dreamed of how good they could become. It's really rewarding for the coach and the athlete."

Know how to fuel: Nothing kills your momentum quicker than a bonk, a condition where energy stores get too low. You'll know you've hit this proverbial wall when the depletion of glycogen stores in your liver and muscles causes a sudden loss of energy and feeling of severe fatigue. Through trial and error, figure out what on-bike foods and drinks work for your stomach, and know how often you need it.

Show your muscle: Use weight training and sprinting to increase the size of your quadriceps and other muscle groups involved in pedaling. For endurance efforts, which are spent mostly in a steady state, you don't need the extra bulk. But to become a better sprinter and improve your power, increasing strength will result in a greater quantity of readily available ATP–PC.

Track progress: Whatever training plan you opt for, make sure to keep track of what you do, how you feel, and how well everything works. This can manifest in all manner of metrics, including mileage and terrain, ride times and workout activity, weather conditions, body weight, race results, and functional threshold power. "The key is logging everything you do so you can go back and learn from it," says Trevor Connor, a longtime cycling coach who also does research in both exercise physiology and nutrition at Colorado State University. "After every ride, make notes of how the ride went, what was going on, what you noticed, how you felt. All that information can help you see longer-term trends for both the good times and bad."

Chapter 21

THE BENEFITS OF TRAINING WITH POWER

It used to be that heart rate was cycling's metric du jour for assessing fitness and dialing in training plans. Max and resting heart rate were determined, training zones were established, and off you went with a heart rate monitor strapped to your chest. But heart rate doesn't always paint a straightforward picture. Heat, hangovers, dehydration, fatigue, and caffeine are just some of the outside environmental factors that can affect heart rate—and none of them have anything to do with how hard or easy you're actually pedaling your bike. Unlike heart rate, the output (displayed in watts) measured by power meters is not influenced by outside factors.

Power meters typically use strain gauges embedded in the crank, hub, pedal, or crank arm spider of your bike. They are designed to measure actual bike rider output in terms of watts. In case you're curious, 746 watts equals 1 horsepower, or about the same output as what a pro level rider exerts to make a sharp but brief attack during a race. Top Tour de France sprinters can hit around 1600 watts upon reaching max speed at the end of a race.

When it comes to training, the value of the power meter is in the truth it tells. No matter how late you stayed out last night or how hot it is, the power meter doesn't care. It provides an exact measure of the work you are doing on the bike, and this information can be incredibly valuable—and motivating—as you try to become a faster cyclist.

"It's a really important tool for me," says multitime US national cyclo-cross champion Jeremy Powers. "It lets me know where I am with my fit-ness. For instance, I know that if I can average 430 watts up a climb for 8 minutes, then I'm in a good place and going well. That is really motivating and confidence-inspiring the next time I line up to race."

Power meters are also a great training tool. Just like with heart rate, you can use one to establish training zones. But instead of resting and max heart rate, your zones will be based on your lactate threshold (LT), which is the max average watts you can produce in a 20-minute, all-out effort (see page 90 for more details). With LT number in hand and training zones deter-mined, it's easy to do effective workouts with prescribed levels of intensity.

"It takes away a lot of the guesswork when you are training," explains Scott Moninger, former pro racer turned coach. "Before I started using one, I'd ride a lot of junk miles that weren't really accomplishing much. But with a power meter, you have a definitive way to quantify what you are doing on your bike."

That might mean doing a series of intervals where you push 400 watts for 30 seconds, then rest for 30 seconds, then repeat. Or you might simply try to keep your power average just under LT during a 1-hour ride. The variations are nearly limitless, and there are entire books dedicated to the art of train-ing with power.

Understanding what it will take to stay at the front of a race during a crit-ical moment is another big benefit derived from using a power meter. Whether it's being able to push that giant 1600-watt number during the final sprint or averaging 350 watts during a race's crucial 5-mile climb, you know ahead of time what you'll be asking your body to do in order to succeed.

"When I was still racing, my coach and I would analyze data and figure out what it took to win an event in a previous year," recalls Moninger. "Then I would have a very specific goal to strive for during training, and if I could get there it gave me a ton of confidence going into the race."

It's worth noting that winning an event is something Moninger did 275 times during his illustrious near two-decade pro racing career.

As valuable as power meters are, though, heart rate should still have a place in your training regimen, says coach Trevor Connor. "Think of a tough

5-hour ride," explains Connor. "Obviously you are going to fatigue, so while maybe you could do 250 watts for 20 minutes no problem at the beginning of the ride, by the end it will be much harder. So, if you were trying to stick to that number, you could end up pushing yourself too hard. Conversely, if you pace using heart rate, it would keep you in the right range of effort."

Bottom line: A power meter is a hugely valuable tool that tells you your actual power output at any given time. And that power output is the metric that ultimately decides who is the fastest rider on any given day.

Chapter 22

DETERMINING YOUR MAX HEART RATE

The previous chapter explained the myriad benefits of training with a power meter. But that doesn't mean a heart rate monitor has no place in your arsenal.

Indeed there is certainly still value in understanding the basics of heart rate training if for no other reason than most heart rate monitors cost less than $100, while a decent power meter will typically set you back at least $500.

For many people, simply riding at a heart rate greater than about 130 beats per minute will ensure some aerobic benefit. But for performance-minded cyclists, the best place to start is with a max heart-rate test. Discovering this maximum is a little painful but worthwhile. It's also worth noting that the alternative formula of "220 minus your age" is notoriously inaccurate. If your pulse is naturally high, then the standard training range recommendations will be too easy. The opposite also applies.

Before taking the test, you'll want to be in at least decent shape. Otherwise you'll tire before actually achieving true maximum heart rate. It's also a good idea to get your doctor's approval.

It's possible to do the test while riding outside. You may even attain your max at the top of a hill during a hard group ride. But doing the test indoors on a stationary trainer provides a better, more-controlled environment.

To do the test you will need a friend to assist you. The goal is to reach your max in about 15 minutes. Shift onto the large chainring and one of the larger rear cogs. Start pedaling and achieve a heart rate of 120 to 130 beats per minute, an easy pace for most riders. Throughout the test, you must maintain a cadence of 80 to 90 revolutions per minute (rpm). Even most basic cycling computers have a cadence function. Otherwise, count pedal strokes for 15 seconds each minute and multiply by four.

Using a heart-rate monitor, have your friend record your heart rate every minute. The monitor consists of two parts: a transmission belt strapped around the chest that relays the heart-rate signal wirelessly, and its receiver, a wristwatch or a device mounted to a handlebar.

The receiver continuously displays the heart rate in beats per minute. An appropriate increase is two or three beats per minute; usually, shifting to the next smaller cog (a higher gear) will get you there. But if you can't get enough resistance on your trainer by using its settings, you can try slightly reducing tire pressure and increasing the roller's pressure against the tread, which in turn will make it harder to pedal.

As you approach your max, your friend is ideally shouting lots of encouragement to continue. Remember, this is a maximal test. It's hard work. It's going to hurt. You must push yourself until you absolutely cannot maintain an 80-plus rpm cadence anymore. At this point, the number on your heart-rate monitor will be a solid approximation of your maximum heart rate. With this number, it's now possible to determine your key heart rate training zones.

Knowing these numbers can help you maintain a heart rate that delivers the most benefit for what you want to accomplish on each ride. Remember

Training Zones

Zone 1: 60 to 70 percent of maximum heart rate = weight loss and endurance building

Zone 2: 70 to 80 percent of maximum heart rate = weight management, improving cardio fitness

Zone 3: 80 to 90 percent of maximum heart rate = interval workouts

Zone 4: Above 90 percent = all-out efforts

that it's just as important to have easy days as it is hard training sessions. Without rest, you won't be able to train hard enough, recover, and grow stronger. Keeping close track of your time on the bike will help you avoid overtraining, which can result in an elevated pulse during easy rides and warmups and poor recovery between intervals. Another sign of overtraining that many cyclists don't recognize is the inability to achieve a high heart rate even though they are riding extremely hard and their legs have a lactic acid burn.

Chapter 23

INTERVAL TRAINING

Intervals, alternating intense hard efforts with easy ones, can be onerous. They hurt, so any enthusiasm that you might initially have probably won't last long, even as you see improvement. For this reason many coaches recommend "recreational" intervals, which will make you better without making you bitter.

As opposed to traditional intervals, the recreational variety has less structure and pressure. With this workout, you simply include several bursts to sustained top speed during the course of one or two rides each week. These are done when the spirit moves you, and the period between each "on" effort can be as long or as short as you like. These won't be quite as effective as structured intervals, but the playfulness means that you are more likely to continue doing them.

Simply stand up out of the saddle, wind up your gear, sit down, and pedal hard for a minute or more. You can create challenges for motivation: Tell yourself to keep going to a specific road sign or to the top of a climb. Then roll easy until you feel like stretching yourself again. It may happen in 2 minutes or 15 minutes. It doesn't make a whole lot of difference, as long as you are surging past your anaerobic threshold several times during the ride.

Of course, some riders prefer more structured intervals. When the schedule says go, you go. When it says stop, you stop. For example, find a moderate incline, stand up out of the saddle, and pedal as hard as you can for 30 seconds. Now coast back down and repeat. Do six efforts, then rest for 10 minutes, and then do another set. For another more structured workout, see the "Interval Workout" sidebar on page 102.

Interval Workout

1. Warm up for at least 15 minutes by spinning along at a moderate pace. Slightly increase intensity during the last few minutes to make sure you are good and ready to go.

2. Now shift into a fairly large gear (say the 53 × 17) that you can spin at 90 to 100 revolutions per minute for the duration of each "on" interval. Stand and sprint to get the gear turning, then sit and push hard for 90 seconds. Your effort should be such that at the end of 90 seconds you need to let off the gas.

3. Shift back to your moderate gear and spin easy for about a minute, letting your heart rate come back down to roughly 60 percent of your max.

4. Immediately shift up and go again, but this time let off after 75 seconds. This shorter work interval allows you to maintain full effort for the duration, despite fatigue from the first effort.

5. Repeat step 3.

6. Continue to alternate big-gear hard riding with moderate-gear easy spinning. Decrease each "on" interval by 15 seconds until you are down to 30 seconds. Then you're done.

7. Cool down with 20 minutes of easy spinning on your way home. Do this once a week for a few months and you'll definitely notice an improvement in your fitness.

HILL CLIMB INTERVALS

Whether you love or loathe climbing, you can't deny the benefit it provides. Pedaling your bike uphill is a surefire way to get fitter and faster. Plus, it means you get to go downhill, which is one of the main reasons we all ride bikes in the first place.

There's nowhere to hide when the road tilts skyward. And even if you don't live in the heart of the Alps or Rockies, you can still improve performance by doing hill intervals. The ideal locale for these type of intervals is a stretch of road about ³⁄₄-mile long, preferably with an uphill grade that takes you 3 to 4 minutes to climb. If you don't have access to any hills, it's okay. An actual hill is not mandatory for this workout, as I'll explain in a moment.

After warming up for 15 to 20 minutes, ride hard to the top of the hill, coast down to recover, then go up again. You may need to do a few loops at the bottom of the hill until your heart rate falls to 60 percent of maximum, which indicates that you have recovered sufficiently. Start out with 4 to 5 reps, then slowly increase over time as you get stronger. Generally speaking, the length of the interval will be about double the recovery period, and the entire session should last 20 to 30 minutes.

A good hill workout also includes gear changes to increase pedaling resistance and improve technique. So, for example, the first time up, use a gear that you can turn fairly easily while seated. The next time, shift down one cog to a harder gear. Then, when you get about 300 feet from the summit, shift down once more, stand, and sprint. Continue to mix it up for the duration of the interval session.

Work on your climbing technique during this training as well. Do not make the common mistake of immediately shifting to lower gears as a hill wears on. At the same time, make sure your cadence is no lower than 75 to 80 rpm. When riding with others, use the lowest gear that lets you keep up with them as the hill starts, while obeying the same cadence rule. Doing this means your legs will be fresh enough to shift to harder gears in the last half of the effort, gaining you speed instead of losing it.

Climbing intervals can also help develop your out-of-saddle riding technique. Immediately before standing, shift to the next smaller cog (higher gear) so that you maintain speed. This is necessary because pedal revolutions decrease when you leave the saddle. Use your body weight to help push the pedals down. Doing this takes upper-body strength plus the coordination that comes only with practice.

As I noted earlier, you do not need an actual hill for this workout, if you happen to ride someplace that is completely devoid of hills. It turns out that you can fake a hill climb workout with a little help from the wind. Do this by pedaling a big gear directly into the wind. The right gear will allow you to achieve a cadence of 80 to 90 revolutions per minute, with a heart rate that nudges just past your lactate threshold by the end, just as it would at the top of a climb. Just as with standard hill intervals, climb for 3 to 4 minutes at a time, recover for roughly the same amount of time, then repeat.

Chapter 24

DOING A TRAINING CAMP

In pro sports, training camps are part of the standard fitness program. That includes cycling teams that gather during each offseason to spin mega miles, building the critical foundation of fitness for the hard days of racing ahead.

But even if Paris-Roubaix or the Tour de France aren't on your to-do list, a training camp can be a great way to jump-start your cycling season. Think of it as a two-wheeled vacation. Pack up your bike and head to a warm locale where you can ride without being bundled up. By spending time solely focusing on riding and recovery, you'll be better able to handle harder efforts down the road, whether it's an amateur racing campaign, long distance gran fondos, or charity rides.

The key to a successful training camp starts with focus, and that means you need to decouple from the rest of life's distractions. Start by getting time off from work. The upcoming days are about riding your bike and relaxing, not staying up late answering e-mails.

Next you'll need to decide if you want to sign up for an organized training camp or put together a do-it-yourself adventure either solo or with a group of riding buddies. If you opt for an organized camp, the options of cost, locale, and services are nearly limitless. Basic US-based camps that include coaching, fully supported rides, and educational seminars typically cost $100 to $125 a day. But you're on your own for lodging and food. Add in room and board and figure you'll need to shell out $300 to $400 a day or more. Luxury tour operator inGamba charges around $1,000 a day plus airfare for weeklong trips in dream destinations such as Tuscany and Portugal.

You'll also want to have at least a baseline of fitness before your camp. If you live in a place where wind chill factor is a lead item on the evening weather forecast, try to spend some time on an indoor trainer before camp. This will help you get the most out of your time at camp, instead of just being in survival mode.

Finally, and most important, you need to have a plan. If you won't be participating in an organized camp, then you (and your riding buddies if you're planning a group affair) need to do some research on the area you'll be riding to figure out the best routes ahead of time. Then, devise a strategy for where you'll ride each day and for how long. And, of course, make sure your bike is tuned up. You don't want to waste your training camp time hanging out at a bike shop waiting for repairs to get done.

Now that we've covered the basics, here's a 7-day program courtesy of coach Frank Overton, owner and founder of FasCat Coaching in Boulder, Colorado.

Day 1: Ride steady tempo for 2 to 3 hours. "Resist the temptation to go too hard or too long," advises Overton. "This first day is just to get the legs warmed up. Cruise around, making sure your bike is ready to go."

Day 2: Now it's time to log some serious miles. "Plan on 2 to 6 hours depending on your current fitness level," says Overton. "And make sure to do a few hard efforts, while at the same time making sure to leave some reserves in the tank. You still have a ways to go."

Day 3: Time for another long day. "Don't go quite as hard or long as the day before," explains Overton. "So if you did 4 to 6 hours the day before, subtract an hour from that for this day's ride. And once again the goal is to ride primarily at a steady tempo pace, mixing in a few hard efforts every hour or so. It doesn't need to be overly structured as long as you get the work in."

Day 4: Rest and relax. Say what, you ask? Well, as almost any coach will tell you, rest is what makes you stronger, because it allows your body to adapt to the increased training load. "You really need to take a day off in the middle of the camp so that you can finish the week strong," says Overton. "I recommend staying off the bike completely. But if you just can't resist, only ride for an hour or so and make sure it's at a casual pace. Cruise over to the coffee shop, get a caffeine fix, and come back. No big chainring at all." Better yet, Overton recommends getting a massage and taking an afternoon nap.

Day 5: Now that you're rested and refreshed, time to get back on the gas with another 4 to 5 hour ride. If possible, opt for a challenging route with some long climbs. "You're trying to push hard on this day," explains Overton.

Day 6: You guessed it, time for another long ride. Follow the same pattern as earlier in the week, slicing about an hour off the total time compared with the day before. "I'd also recommend having an alternative shorter route just in case you get on the bike and realize you're too tired to go big again," says Overton.

Day 7: Massive fatigue is surely setting in now—and you likely have to travel the next day—so opt for a lower intensity ride that's somewhere between 90 minutes and 3 hours.

By the end of these 7 days, you are going to be tired, and that means it's time to rest. Overton recommends taking at least 3 to 4 days off the bike. "You're going to be smoked and your body is going to need time to recuperate," he adds. "But get excited for the rides ahead. You've put the work in and will definitely notice performance gains."

Chapter 25

TIPS FOR TRAINING INDOORS

Training indoors . . . for most cyclists it's a necessary evil at some point in the year. But indoor trainer time doesn't have to be a mind-numbing, soul-crushing experience. Indeed, riding the trainer can actually be a great way to get some serious on-bike work done in a relatively short amount of time. And, done right, three or four weekly rides to nowhere can actually increase your power and speed. Here are some tips to making training time pass quickly.

Don't skimp: Sure, you can find a trainer on the Internet for $99, but odds are high that you will get what you pay for. In other words, don't be afraid to invest a little. A good trainer will provide years of use. Budget trainers will feel like you are pedaling through sand, while a higher-end model will provide a more realistic road feel. Also check out the wide array of indoor training-specific apps and videos. The amount of boredom-squashing stimulation you can get these days is amazing.

Get some air: You will generate an enormous amount of body heat on an indoor trainer. Create an artificial headwind by placing a fan in front of your bike. You'll also want to keep a towel handy for wiping away sweat. If possible, ride in a room that has some natural air circulation.

Drink up: Fluids are important to keep your core temperature down and to replace the energy you're burning (this applies whether you are indoors or on the road). Drink at least one 16-ounce bottle of your sports drink of choice during a 45-minute indoor session.

Be brief: There's no reason to grind away on the trainer for hours on end.

You can get a great indoor workout in less than an hour. Wait until you are back outside to do those long rides.

Change it up: Beat boredom by doing something different every minute or two. Stand up, change gears, increase your cadence, alternate hand positions, pedal with one foot while resting the other on a stool—anything to add variety and help make the time go faster.

Look and/or listen: Some riders prefer listening to podcasts or music, while others like watching TV. Regardless, find something entertaining that will help take your mind off the fact that you are pedaling to nowhere.

Change your shorts: If you're trying to do a long workout (more than an hour), consider swapping on a clean kit each hour. No one likes the feel of a sweat-soaked chamois, and just being able to get off the bike and changing clothes will make you feel refreshed and energized for the remainder of your workout.

Take care of busy work: Indoor workouts are a great place for things such as pedaling drills, one-leg drills, high cadence, low cadence, and all the other little things you'd rather not do when riding outside. One of the best drills is one-leg, where you really focus on pedaling smooth circles. Do this for 1 to 3 minutes, then switch legs. If you've never done them before, you will quickly realize how uneven your stroke is and how weak that hamstring is when pulling up on the pedal; most cyclists tend to just push down.

Increase cadence: High cadence is another great drill to do while riding the trainer. For example, do 5 minutes at 120 rpm. You likely have a cadence sweet spot of around 85 or 90 rpm, and while riding outdoors you may not vary much from it. Drills such as this force you out of that comfort zone and can improve the overall smoothness of your pedal stroke.

Try rollers: For a true pedaling action feel, spend some time on a set of stationary rollers. Because they more closely replicate riding outdoors, you can't just zone out. However, if you are doing a set of hard intervals where you need to focus on power output or heart rate, use the trainer. Also remember when on the rollers to make sure you are next to something you can grab. Crashing on rollers is not fun.

Use a power meter: If you have access to a power meter, use it. Measuring power is key for indoor workouts. It's an absolute gauge of the amount of work you are doing, and it gives you something to focus on during your workout. Heart rate is an acceptable second choice, but you will find that heart rate varies a lot with cadence, meaning that power is a much better tool for maximizing the quality of an indoor riding session.

Try this workout: Using a power meter, play with your cadence by doing a power tempo workout. Start in the 53 × 11 (or whatever your hardest gear is) and ride for 5 minutes while maintaining an even power output. Then shift to one gear easier and do another 5 minutes at the same power. Continue shifting to an easier gear every 5 minutes, always trying to maintain the same power output. This is a good way to mix things up and keep your ride interesting. You get more from a workout when you get out of your comfort zone.

Take a class: Last but certainly not least, consider taking an indoor cycling class. It can be really motivating to be around other people, and a good instructor will be able to provide structure to your workout, help you set goals, and encourage you to work toward achieving them.

Chapter 26

LOSING WEIGHT

Road cycling is famous for riders who spare no expense to lighten their bikes (and often their wallets). Lusting after featherweight carbon fiber gear can be a very expensive hobby. And while it's always helpful to shave off a little weight, the best place to start is on your body—not your bike. Trimming a few pounds will help your performance by improving your power-to-weight ratio. Of course it's also good for overall health and appearance, too. And the good news is that you don't have to forgo your favorite foods in order to lose weight. Here are some tips for unpacking that extra baggage you have been carrying around.

Don't rely solely on diets: Yes, you lose weight when you cut calories, but all of the lost poundage isn't fat. A significant percentage of weight loss—up to 30 percent—comes from muscle tissue. Cyclists on a diet often end up thinner, but become slower and weaker on the bike. As pioneering diet expert Covert Bailey wrote, "When someone says that they lost 20 pounds, the key question is: 20 pounds of what?" Some dieters can end up having a higher percentage of body fat even as they lose weight. And don't forget that muscle burns calories. The more muscle volume you have, the more calories your body consumes. If you lose muscle, you will gain fat faster when you return to your pre-diet eating habits.

Ride, ride, ride: The average road cyclist burns about 40 calories per mile. At a relatively sedate 15 miles per hour, this means a weekly time commitment of 10 hours on the bike can burn a whopping 6,000 calories.

Boost carbs, trim fat: Your problem may not be how much you eat but the nutritional balance among carbohydrate, fat, and protein. For high-level endurance performance, aim for 60 to 70 percent carbohydrate with less than 30 percent fat. This will also help with weight loss. It usually isn't necessary to make radical adjustments to achieve these percentages. Small changes work best. For instance, don't eat a whole bowl of chili with meat. Instead fill half the bowl with brown rice, then ladle a small amount of chili on top. Try substituting fat-free yogurt for sour cream and fruit for sweets.

Keep your upper body fit: Because cycling is primarily a leg sport, riders can lose muscle volume in their upper body. This is important, remember, because if you lose muscle, you don't burn as many calories. The solution is year-round resistance training. But this doesn't mean hours in the weight room. As little as 20 minutes twice a week during the cycling season, and 30 minutes two or three times weekly during the winter, will maintain and even increase your upper body muscle mass. (For more information on weight training, see Chapter 27.)

Go long and easy: Take a long, slow ride once a week, especially in the early season. Long rides (up to 6 hours) burn a lot of fat and give you a good endurance base for later in the season.

Recharge properly: Recovery matters. After a ride, you need to refuel with plenty of carbohydrates. Don't think that you'll lose weight faster if you don't eat. You'll just get weak and not feel well. Also, be sure to take recovery rides that are slow and easy.

Embrace the peak: Your weight will vary. Jeremy Powers, multi-time US national cyclocross champion, understands just how his weight will fluctuate during the racing season. "I will get my weight really low for a certain target event, but then come off that number by 3 or 4 pounds afterward," says Powers. "I basically do blocks of not eating much, and then ease off. It's all about give-and-take and finding balance."

Fill up on water: To ride enough in summer heat to lose weight, you must stay hydrated. Be sure that you start summertime rides with at least two full bottles, and know where you can stop for refills along the way.

Short rides can still do the trick: Even 40 minutes of cycling can help you lose weight if you go hard.

Eat in moderation: Cut fat and eat more vegetables, but don't go overboard. Moderation is important. If you have a sweet tooth, eat some candy or dessert once in a while. If you always deprive yourself, you might binge. You also need to be honest with yourself about what you are eating, says Frank Overton, owner and founder of Boulder, Colorado's FasCat Coaching. "There is so much crap that people have in their diet that is just out of habit," says Overton. "Try to reduce or cut out soda, sugar, junk food. Have a few less beers each week, or drink wine since it typically has fewer calories."

Don't stuff yourself: Stop eating before you are full. You don't need to feel stuffed after every meal. "It's okay to feel a little hungry," says Overton. "That doesn't mean starve yourself or skip meals. But if you can cut 500 calories a day, you will lose about a pound a week."

Do a dietary recall: Overton also suggests trying to keep track of everything you put in your mouth for one week. "There are lots of good apps that can help with this," he says. "So you log everything for a week, and then analyze it and try to figure out what you could cut out. You'll be surprised at what you find."

Get a plan: If you don't want to go it alone, get help from a certified nutritionist, who can help you come up with a meal plan that will help you lose weight without going to extreme measures. There are also many online groups and forums that you can join for virtual support.

Increase your pep: Have faith that as you drop weight, you will gain more pep. Exercise raises your energy level. Once you get used to the idea of riding, it becomes easier to get out there. It's a reward in itself and really makes you feel rejuvenated.

Chapter 27
WEIGHT TRAINING

You have heard all the excuses for not lifting weights. It takes too much time. Gym memberships are expensive. But weight training can greatly improve your on-bike performance.

Pumping iron isn't good for just riding and racing either. Lifting weights helps retain muscle volume as you age so that you can ride fast and strong over the years. Added strength also protects against injury. Best of all is that it only takes a few hours each week. During winter, lift 2 or 3 days each week and aim for strength gains. To retain the strength you have built as you begin riding more in the spring, lift once or twice per week and don't worry about pushing the intensity. Here are some more tips and tricks to get the most out of your weight-lifting routine.

Use proper form: To avoid injury, do all exercises correctly. If you don't know how, consider hiring a personal trainer to help you. Alternatively, spend some time researching on the Internet, which is a vast resource of information.

Do your homework: If time and/or money is an issue, work out at home to increase convenience and decrease expense. For many exercises, your body is the only weight you need. Add a chinup bar, light barbell set, bench, and a sturdy platform for stepups, and you can work virtually any muscle group.

Time it right: Lift after easy rides when you are warmed up but not tired. Include gentle stretching. About 20 minutes in winter and 10 to 15 minutes in summer will suffice for the whole routine.

Get a leg up on training: During spring and summer, riding usually provides enough work for your legs. If you want more, try squats on the bike, using a slightly larger than normal gear on climbs or when riding into the

Year-Round Strength Training Routine

Adhere to the progressive resistance principle. That is, as your body adapts to a training load, you must increase resistance to continue improving. When you can do a set of 10 to 12 repetitions of an exercise comfortably, increase the amount of weight, the number of reps, or the number of sets.

Strengthening Phase: November through March

Two or three times per week (but not on consecutive days), do one to three sets in each of these five areas.

1. Upper-body pushing exercise, such as pushups, bench presses, or dips
2. Upper-body pulling exercise, such as pullups, bent rows, or upright rows
3. Abdominal exercise, such as crunches
4. Lower-back exercise, such as back extensions
5. Leg exercise, such as stepups, lunges, or light squats

Maintenance Phase: April through October

Two times per week (preferably after an easy ride), do one set in each of these four areas.

1. Upper-body pushing, such as pushups, bench presses, or dips
2. Upper-body pulling, such as pullups, bent rows, or upright rows
3. Abdominal exercises, such as crunches
4. Lower-back exercises, such as back extensions

wind. (Be sure to warm up carefully before doing this and don't try it if you have knee problems.) In winter, simple exercises, such as lunges and stepups, can keep your quadriceps strong while you cross-train with running, Nordic skiing, or other aerobic activities.

Remember the reason: You're a cyclist, not a Mr. Universe contestant. Don't forget this. Regularity beats volume. It's better to lift a little each week for the rest of your life than overdose on iron, get injured, and quit.

Try this: A streamlined weight-training program won't result in bulging biceps and six-pack abs. But it will improve cycling performance. See the sidebar "Year-Round Strength Training Routine" on the previous page.

Chapter 28

GETTING READY FOR YOUR FIRST CENTURY RIDE

Now that you have a basic understanding of how the body works and have learned some of the most popular training techniques, it's time to set a goal and put a plan of action in place. Among the most common first big goals for new cyclists is the century ride. Whether your chosen event raises money for charity or simply provides the infrastructure and support for riders to have a good (and safe) time challenging themselves, riding a 100-miler is a rite of passage in the two-wheeled world.

But covering that great a distance by bike isn't something you want to try straight off the proverbial couch. Indeed, you need a plan that will help get you to the finish line. "The good news is that if you are a new cyclist, your slope of improvement will be exceptionally high," says coach Frank Overton, owner and founder of FasCat Coaching in Boulder, Colorado. "Just riding more will lead to rapid improvement."

At the same time, Overton recommends carefully tracking your progress. A simple way to start is to take what you did one week and add half that much more each ensuing week. So if you rode 2 hours this week, do 3 hours next week, and so on. Just remember to back off if you start to feel overly tired or experience overuse injury symptoms such as knee pain.

"And when you start planning, think in terms of weeks and months and then drill down to days," advises Overton. "So a simple plan would be to ride more in the spring than the winter, and more in the summer than the spring."

That could mean in January riding your bike two to three times a week for 30 to 50 minutes, and then keep adding days, aiming to get to three to four times a week in February, and then four to five times a week in March and so on.

Coach Trevor Connor prescribes to a similar strategy, focusing on endurance rather than intensity. "With a new athlete the key is getting them to the finish line, not winning the event. That comes later," Connor says. "So, initially, I would aim for doing a lot of base work, where volume is the key."

To achieve this, Connor likes to jump-start the process with what he calls a training camp structure. His athletes log 3 to 4 consecutive weeks of riding 3 days in a row, starting with 1 to 2 hours a day and increasing from there. "The initial key is getting the person to the point of being able to do a 5 to 6 hour ride, because that is what the century ride will be like," adds Connor.

Of course many new cyclists don't have time to log that many hours on the bike. Family and work get in the way. That's where shorter rides with more intensity come in. Among the most popular approaches when time is tight is a concept pioneered by Overton called sweet spot training.

"The idea of sweet spot training is to get the most out of the time on your bike," explains Overton. "Sweet spot training balances intensity and volume. That's why it's called sweet spot."

Overton says a rider's sweet spot resides between high zone 3 and low zone 4 (see the "Training Zones" sidebar in Chapter 22), or roughly between 85 percent and 95 percent of their functional threshold power or FTP, which is the highest average watts (measured by a power meter) a rider can produce during an all-out, 1-hour effort. (For explanations and details, see Chapters 21 and 22.) Athletes who have a power meter use FTP to set their training zones, which are all based on a percentage of their FTP. If you don't have a power meter, Overton says think of your sweet spot as riding "medium hard."

Once you have figured out your sweet spot, try spending as much time there as possible when you ride, advises Overton. "Go out and ride hard but not super hard," he adds, advising to keep your initial effort around 90 to 95 percent of your FTP. "Get after it, and as you fatigue let your wattage fall, accepting the fatigue that comes with riding hard but not going so hard that you won't be able to do it again the next day."

That repeatable balance between intensity and volume is what will elicit the most adaptation (aka increased fitness).

"If you could do threshold work all the time, that would be different," adds Overton. "But the key with sweet spotting is that it allows the athlete's body to recover and therefore repeat and achieve similar wattages day after day with more frequency than full-on threshold workouts. And, ultimately, the end result is a higher power at threshold, which is what we're all striving for, whether it's riding a century or trying to win a race."

Part Six

FUELING YOUR RIDE

Chapter 29

HYDRATE OR DIE

When it comes to on-bike fueling, nothing is more important than staying properly hydrated. The main "ingredient" of your blood is water, so if you lose body water, your blood volume drops. That means you don't get enough blood to the muscles. And when you lose blood flow to muscles, you lose power.

This is underscored by the fact that your body loses fluids quickly during periods of intense physical exertion, especially in high temperature conditions. In extreme cases, it's possible to sweat out more than 2 quarts per hour, and a total fluid loss of 8 percent of body weight can occur in just a few hours. If you happen to be riding in humid conditions, that loss is accelerated because evaporative cooling slows.

In addition, when you're as little as a quart low on fluids, your ability to sweat is reduced and body temperature rises—and this can lead to poor performance on the bike. Studies have shown that fluid losses of as little as 2 percent of body weight significantly reduce high-intensity cycling performance from start to exhaustion. Simply put, if you're dehydrated, you'll be slower on your bike. To avoid that, follow these tips.

Drink plenty of fluids: This is the most basic of cycling tenets. Hydrate before, during, and after rides. Practice drinking more than you want; thirst will not inadequately stimulate you to completely rehydrate. Drink fluids before you are thirsty. Aim for at least 16 ounces per hour when riding, or better yet try to down one standard-size water bottle, which is 22 ounces, because that amount is easier to track.

Drink more than water: While H_2O is the basic sustainer of life on planet Earth, cyclists need more than just water to keep going strong. There are literally hundreds of hydration products on the market, starting with basic Gatorade and expanding from there. Choosing the product that works best for you is a highly individual process. Just remember that race (or event) day is not the time to be experimenting with a new product. No matter what you choose, make sure it's something you'll be able to drink for an extended period of time. Sometimes the sweet, sticky taste of these drinks gets hard to swallow, especially when a drink gets warm. One trick is to freeze half a bottle of sports drink overnight and then top it off before the ride. Cooler drinks are typically easier on the stomach, not to mention the psyche.

Skip the hyper-hydration routine: Inevitably at big cycling events, you'll see riders gulping copious amounts of fluid before the ride or race. While it would be nice if we could "stock up" like this, the best advice is simply not to be dehydrated, advises Matt Pahnke, PhD, a principal scientist for the Gatorade Sports Science Institute. "Don't be the guy carrying around the gallon jug of water," Dr. Pahnke says. "You'll just be up all night going to bathroom."

Weigh yourself: As you've no doubt heard many times before, no two humans are exactly alike. This adage applies to fluid loss, too. According to Dr. Pahnke, there is a significant variation in the amount of fluid and sodium people lose during exercise. He recommends that each athlete determine how much fluid they lose. To do this, he suggests using body weight as a gauge of hydration status and how much you are sweating.

First warm up, then weigh yourself. Now ride for 30 to 60 minutes and weigh yourself again. Essentially all that will have changed in body weight is due to fluid loss. Ideally, you'll want to run this test at various intensity levels and climates (hot day, cold day). Once that's done, you'll have a general idea of how much fluid you are losing each hour. If your fluid loss is more than 2 to 3 percent of your body weight, you will start to experience negative effects. (For reference, a pound equates to about 16 ounces of fluid.) Now that you know your approximate sweat rate, try to match that with fluid intake. This won't be possible for some riders who lose a lot of fluid, because there's simply a limit to how much fluid you can empty from your stomach and absorb into your body without causing gastrointestinal issues. But you want to get as close as you can.

While we all need water to live, cyclists need a little something more
if they want to perform at their peak.

Pay attention to your pee: While there is no one-size-fits-all answer to how much water you should drink per day, an easy way to monitor your level of hydration is to keep an eye on the color of your urine. If it's darker yellow, you need to drink more. If it's pale, you're doing well. Need help remembering what's what? Just remember the phrase, "A happy mountaineer always pees clear."

Dress appropriately: The cycling apparel industry has created all manners of materials that claim to keep you cool on the bike. Without passing judgment on these so-called wonder garments, simply try a cycling kit that helps combat the effects of a hot summer day. Typically this means slipping on light-colored clothing, which reflects rather than absorbs sunlight. For the same reason, wear a well-ventilated helmet (bonus points if it's light colored). Also look for cycling shorts made from wicking materials, which help sweat evaporate quicker to enhance cooling.

Know how to drink: Obviously, the ability to tip a cup to your mouth is a skill you likely mastered sometime before your second birthday. But drinking in general and drinking while riding a bike are two totally different animals. And if you haven't mastered the latter, odds are high you'll end up dehydrated simply because you didn't drink enough. To avoid this, practice reaching down and grabbing your water bottle while on the move. If you're nervous, practice this skill on a stationary trainer to start. Once you feel more comfortable, head out onto the open road.

Get acclimated: If you live in a place where the climate is cooler and drier (Colorado, for example), and your next race is in a hot and humid place (say, Florida), do your best to get prepared for the change in heat and humidity. Scott Moninger, former pro racer turned coach, offers some advice. "For instance, it was almost always super hot at the US Pro Championships in Philadelphia," says Moninger, who was based in more temperate Colorado during his racing career. "I would always try to get out there a few days ahead of time, just to let my body get used to those conditions. It's the same thing a flatlander would want to do if they were coming to Colorado to race at altitude."

Chapter 30

HOW TO FIND THE RIGHT HYDRATION PRODUCT FOR YOU

Which sports drink is the best? There is no right answer. Just individual preferences. What tastes great and works well for one person is a stomach-ache in the making for another. So what do you do? Test, test, and test some more until you find the right concoction for you and your performance needs. Here are some tips that will help you down that path of discovery.

Follow protocol: If you have the available time, it's best to spread out test sessions by about a week. Also make sure to try to do the exact same things leading up to each test ride. That means eating the same food, getting the same amount of sleep, and following the same pre-hydration routine. You'll also want to do each test at the same time of day. Finally, make sure you match calorie consumption. So if one drink is a food-in-a-bottle product and the next is hydration only, you'll need to compensate for that difference by eating blocks, gels, or whatever else will fit in your jersey pocket. (Just make sure you have pretested the food and know that it won't upset your stomach.)

Do a repeatable effort: When it comes time for your test ride, whether it's a hill climb or flat time trial effort, make sure you ride the same course each time. During the test, record key metrics such as heart rate and power output, as well as more subjective measures such as how your stomach and legs felt. Then analyze that information when making the final call.

Trust your gut: The number-one thing a hydration product should not do is make you feel like crap. But as any experienced cyclist will tell you, there are products out there that just don't pass the test. If you wouldn't be comfortable using a product while hanging out at the house all day, chances are slim that it will work while you're out on a long bike ride. Exercise can be stressful on your gastrointestinal system. If a drink product turns your stomach into knots when you're not under the stress of exercise, it is unlikely that same product will make you feel good during your next century ride or criterium race.

The day after: In addition to documenting your day-of test session metrics, keep track of how recovery goes. Did you suffer from any post-ride stomach discomfort? Did you sleep well? These are factors that should be tallied up when making a final judgment on how well a product works for you.

Check the scale: Weigh yourself before and after each ride. When a product works well for you, it typically means you drank more and thus didn't lose as much weight through fluid loss. This is an extremely valuable metric because it indicates an improvement in hydration (or decrease in dehydration), which will almost certainly lead to an improvement in performance.

Chapter 31

BASIC NUTRITION TIPS

In most recreational sports, eating is something you do afterward. You don't see LeBron James wolfing down a sandwich at halftime or Mike Trout nibbling on rice cakes between innings. But in cycling, eating is an important part of success while actually participating in the sport. For any ride longer than 90 minutes, you will need to replenish calories along with fluids. This is news to a lot of beginning riders. It is even occasionally overlooked by experienced cyclists, who start their day aiming for the podium or a personal best but end up bonking. Here are the basics that you need to know when it comes to eating on the bike.

Food is fuel: Food—be it gels, bars, or a turkey sandwich stuffed in your jersey pocket—replenishes the energy you burn while pedaling. Every time you eat something, your body takes the food's carbohydrate (natural compounds derived from starches and sugars) and stores it as fuel (glycogen) in your muscles. You have enough stored glycogen to provide energy for short rides, typically 90 minutes or less. But for longer efforts, you need to eat along the way or your glycogen stores become depleted. When this occurs, less fuel reaches your brain and muscles, and you feel dizzy and tired. Yes, you have bonked.

Eat before you are hungry: Don't wait until hunger pains set in to grab a bite of that bar in your back pocket. If you wait for your body to tell you that it needs nourishment, the energy won't be able to reach your muscles fast enough to help. Instead, nibble during your ride to keep a steady flow of fuel coming in. This is better than stuffing yourself at mid-ride rest stops. Gorging puts stress on your body because your digestive system requires blood to process food, which means that less blood will be available for delivering oxygen to your muscles.

What to eat: No surprise here—once again there is no right answer. You need to figure out what works for you. Some riders can slurp energy gels all day. Others need something with a little more substance. There is even a contingent of cyclists who, come race day, take in all their food in liquid form via all-in-one hydration drinks that deliver calories along with hydration. The one thing you do want to avoid are fat and fiber, which can slow down digestion. This translates into less fuel getting delivered to your muscles.

How to eat: Of course you know how to eat. Sit down at the dining room table, pick up a fork, and go to work. But eating on the bike is a different story. If you're not in a race or trying to achieve a personal best, then there is no harm in pulling off to the side of the road and taking a break. But if dashing across the finish line first is your goal, then you will need to be able to eat on the fly.

The best place to carry food is in one of the rear pockets of your jersey. Figure out which side works best and pack accordingly. Put essential items (such as food) in the pocket you are most comfortable reaching into while riding. When it comes time to pull out that energy bar, first grip the handlebar with one hand near the stem to hold the bike steady. Then reach around with your other hand and grab what you need. Or, if you are confident in your abilities, ride no-handed for a minute so that you can grab your food and get it into your mouth. One great trick is to unwrap items before your ride so you don't have to deal with pesky packaging while on the go.

Grab a cold one: The stomach empties faster with cool liquids than it does with warm or air-temperature ones. Also, sugar and electrolytes improve taste. It's easy to prove this to yourself. After a long, hot ride, look at a warm jug of water. Then consider a big, refrigerated bottle of sports drink. Which is more appealing?

Learn what works for you: Use training rides to determine what works for you. Never experiment before or during a big event.

Shape up: Training improves your stomach's ability to function at a given workload. In other words, if you are fit, a smaller percentage of your oxygen uptake is required by working muscles, which in turn allows more oxygen to be available for digestion in the GI tract.

Chapter 32

CONVENIENCE-STORE CALORIES

By now you've surely figured out that your energy supply must be restocked after a couple of hours of cycling. That is roughly how long it takes to exhaust your carbohydrate stores. But what if you already devoured the contents of your jersey pockets and still have another 100 miles to ride?

Well maybe you just happen to be riding past a Whole Foods Market. But odds are that the next store you pass will be a convenience store. Normally you might never eye the local Quickie Mart as a source of quality sustenance. But in a pinch, especially when you're trying to stave off a bonk, you can actually find what you need in a convenience store.

Yes, though traditionally considered nutritional junkyards, these emporiums of empty calories are actually carbohydrate gold mines in disguise. You just need to know which foods to choose. Scan the aisles carefully and you will find an assortment of high-octane fuels, ranging from microwaveable burritos to energy bars to sports drinks. The key is to look for foods containing at least 60 percent carbohydrate and no more than 30 percent fat. Here is a shopping list to get you started.

Chicken burritos: Many convenience stores have microwave ovens for heating up the packaged burritos you will find in the cooler section. Not all burritos are created equal. Many are stuffed with fat. So before you key in your cook time, read the nutrition label. Try to find one that hits the 60 percent carbohydrate sweet spot.

Fruit-flavored yogurt: Stroll over to the dairy cooler in search of this deluxe carb-packed item. Ideally try to find a yogurt of the low-fat variety.

A typical 1-cup serving of low-fat yogurt contains about 250 calories, with 45 grams of carbohydrate (15 percent), 10 grams of protein, and 2.5 grams of fat (4 percent). Combine the yogurt with a single-serving box of cereal to up the flavor—and carbohydrate—quotient.

Fig bars: This cycling standby is common in convenience stores, easy to eat, and agreeable to the stomach. And they contain little fat. Typically two bars provide about 140 calories, 32 grams of carbohydrate (11 percent), 2 grams of protein, and 2 grams of fat (3 percent).

Fruit: You will usually have to pay out the nose for fruit at convenience stores as compared to grocery stores, but the price is worth it: real fruit is great for a carb refuel, and each piece comes loaded with lots of vitamins and minerals. A banana has about 100 calories, an apple about 80, and an orange about 60. None contain significant amounts of fat or protein.

Corn nuts: Some cyclists crave salt rather than sugar when their energy runs low. If this includes you, do yourself a favor: Skip the potato chips, which are often more than 50 percent fat. Instead look for some corn nuts. They will satisfy your salty desires and deliver about 20 grams of carbohydrate (7 percent) in 130 calories, 2 grams of protein, and 4 grams of fat (6 percent). You will also likely find bags of peanuts, almonds or nut mixes that will help re-up your fuel stores.

Pretzels: Another good alternative to chips, a 2-ounce serving of pretzels typically delivers about 220 calories, 44 grams of carbohydrate (15 percent), 6 grams of protein, and 2 grams of fat (3 percent).

V8 juice: Mom always said eat your vegetables, and V8 Vegetable Juice lets you drink them. This cold beverage is primarily tomato juice mixed with other veggies. It contains more vitamins and minerals than many sports drinks and has significant amounts of antioxidants, which are nutrients that help your body eliminate destructive free radicals. Slam back an 8-ounce serving, and you get 150 percent daily value for vitamin C and 40 percent for vitamin A. You will also benefit from 50 calories, 10 grams of carbohydrate, 2 grams of protein, and no fat.

PayDay bar: If you must succumb to the urge to indulge in a candy bar, opt for a PayDay bar, which is more than just a gooey mass of high fructose corn syrup. A normal size bar has 240 calories, 110 of which come from fat. But you will also get 27 grams of carbohydrates and 7 grams of protein. For comparison sake, a chocolate chip flavored Clif Bar has 250 calories, with 45 calories coming from fat, plus 45 grams of carbohydrates and 10 grams of protein. Of course Clif Bars are made almost entirely of organic ingredients, while the ingredient list on a PayDay nutrition information label includes the likes of sugar, corn syrup, vegetable oil, and something called diglycerides.

Chapter 33

10 KEY FUELING FACTS AND TIPS

You know how it feels to shop in an unfamiliar grocery store? Confusing, huh? Well, the world of nutrition is similarly convoluted. Today's life-saving diet is tomorrow's unfounded fad. Like riding with your faster friends, it's difficult to keep up. And while it's impossible to clear up all that confusion, having a baseline of useful information is always helpful. Here then are 10 key fueling facts and tips that will help you better navigate these murky waters so that you can more effectively feed and drink on the fly.

1. Water is your friend: Although it doesn't supply calories, vitamins, or minerals, water is essential for virtually every bodily function. It aids digestion, cushions organs, and keeps your body temperature from rising to lethal levels during exercise. In fact, H_2O is so important that it accounts for 55 to 65 percent of your weight.

2. Cycling is hot: When you are cycling, your muscles produce up to 100 times more heat than when you are at rest. The body extinguishes this inferno primarily by increasing your sweat rate. On a really hot day you can lose more than 2 liters (about 67 ounces) of fluids per hour when exercising. If you don't replace these fluids, your power output declines quickly. One study of trained cyclists found that without fluids they could barely finish a 2-hour ride at 65 percent of maximum oxygen capacity.

3. Less H_2O = more beats: Studies by Edward Coyle, PhD, director of the Human Performance Laboratory at the University of Texas at Austin, reveal that cyclists who lose a quart of fluid experience a rise in heart rate of eight beats per minute, a decrease in cardiac function, and an increase in body temperature. Dehydration, says Dr. Coyle, may cause increased metabolic stress on muscles and faster glycogen depletion. It also wreaks havoc on your internal thermostat by decreasing blood flow to the skin, slowing your sweat rate, and increasing the time needed for fluids to be absorbed into the blood stream. What's worse, by the time you feel thirsty, your body has already lost up to 2 percent of its weight—about a quart of fluid.

4. Drink, drink, drink: The popular notion of drinking eight 8-ounce glasses of fluids daily is easy to remember, but may not be right for you. Indeed, people have different fluid needs depending on fitness, gender, body size, and environmental conditions. Your best bet is to gauge hydration by monitoring six simple markers.

Do you urinate less than three times during a normal day? Is your urine dark yellow? Does it have a strong odor? Do you get headaches toward the end of a long ride or shortly afterward? Do you drink less than one water bottle per hour while riding? Do you lose more than 2 pounds during rides? If you answer yes to any of these questions, your body is heading for a drought. Time to start drinking more until the situation is rectified.

5. Set a schedule: To negate fluid loss via sweat, practice drinking strategies during training. Determine your sweat rate per hour by weighing yourself before and after rides. (Every pound lost equals about 16 ounces of fluid.) Then figure out how much fluid your stomach can tolerate per hour and determine the best drinking schedule to replace it. Set an alarm to alert you to drink 4 to 8 ounces every 15 minutes, regardless of whether you feel thirsty.

6. Replenish your supply: After you have ridden for several hours, pump down more fluids. What you drink makes a difference. In a study conducted by Dr. Coyle, dehydrated athletes were asked to drink nearly 2 liters of fluid 2 hours after they exercised. The catch is that these athletes drank diet cola, water, or a sports drink. The study then compared the quality of replenishment each provides. Dr. Coyle found that diet cola replenished 54 percent of the fluid loss; water, 64 percent; and sports drink, 69 percent.

7. Snack on something salty: Sodium makes your blood sponge-like, allowing you to absorb more water and excrete less. Each liter of sweat saps between 500 and 1,000 (or more) milligrams of sodium.

8. Choose juicy foods: Around 60 percent of your daily fluid comes from the foods you eat, but some foods increase hydration better than others. For instance, fruits and vegetables are great fluid sources; they are 80 to 95 percent water by weight. Eating the recommended five to nine daily servings of produce means that you will get a lot of extra water in your diet. If you are downing protein supplements, you should drink even more water, as you will need that additional water to metabolize and excrete the extra protein.

9. Be a sport: Most popular sports hydration drinks contain sodium, potassium, and other electrolytes as well as energy-producing carbohydrate. These drinks are recommended for exercise that lasts more than an hour. Whenever you plan to cycle for several hours, make sure you carry two bottles. In addition, have a plan to fill up along the way. Whichever brand of sports drink you choose, make sure you like the way it tastes so that you'll be motivated to drink. Also, cool fluids taste better and may be absorbed more rapidly than warm ones.

10. Try beet juice: Sure, we may someday find out this was just a fad, but there is growing evidence that nitrates such as those found in beet juice can help boost aerobic performance, says Matt Pahnke, PhD, a principal scientist for the Gatorade Sports Science Institute. It's shown some benefits as far as improving efficiency, meaning that the same amount of work requires less oxygen. And that is obviously a good thing.

Chapter 34

RECOVERY IS KEY

It's widely accepted that what you do (or, more precisely, what you put in your body) during the first 30 minutes after an intense ride plays a significant role in how well your body will recover. By ingesting some protein right away, you shut down the production of cortisol, the stress hormone that causes the breakdown of protein, which enables you to fuel yourself while riding.

The sooner you can halt the production of cortisol, the better you will feel when you go out and ride again the next day. Recovery also influences your overall energy level going forward. As any bike riding regular knows, when you don't recover well, you typically don't feel particularly well the following day, a feeling often called the bicycle hangover. So what is the ideal way to bounce back and be ready for your next big ride? Follow these tips.

Start fast: Getting something into your body in those first 30 minutes after intense exercise is key. And if you can do it right away, that's even better, says Matt Pahnke, PhD, a principal scientist for the Gatorade Sports Science Institute. "This is when protein becomes really important," explains Dr. Pahnke. "About 20 grams is the recommendation, but how you get that protein is up to you. Some people opt for one of the ubiquitous recovery drink products that flood the endurance-sports market. But better yet, eat some real food, such as a turkey sandwich, chicken fried rice, or a yogurt smoothie with fruit. Even chugging a coke is better than nothing. Just make sure you do something in those first 30 minutes."

Cool down: Once you've gotten some protein into your system, take a shower to help cool down your body temperature. This is another key step in the recovery process, says Allen Lim, PhD, a sports physiologist and cycling coach, who once served as director of sport science for both Garmin and RadioShack cycling teams. "When body temperature is high, it stays catabolic and continues to be in that mode of exercise," adds Dr. Lim. "You need to bring it back to normal to start the process of rebuilding."

Get compressed: Give your muscles an added boost by slipping on a pair of compression socks, or go all out and spend some time hooked up to a pair of compression boots. In each case, pressure is tightest at the ankles and gradually becomes less constrictive toward the knees and thighs. These devices compress the surface veins, arteries, and muscles. The circulating blood is forced through narrower circulatory channels, which in turn results in increased arterial pressure, causing more blood to return to the heart and less blood to pool in the feet.

Snack a lot: After a particularly hard ride, it's a good idea get another hit of protein about 2 hours afterward. This helps keep muscle repair going and boosts the immune system. In general, when training hard you are better off having four or five small meals per day than the traditional three square meals. Dr. Pahnke suggests aiming for 20 grams of protein every 3 to 4 hours.

Snack before bed: Before you head off to the land of dreams, have one more small meal to keep the recovery process going. Options for a bedtime snack include a small bowl of Greek yogurt with a couple of berries on top, or a few slices of turkey meat, which have the added benefit of containing the amino acid tryptophan, which is a natural sedative.

Be yourself: This cannot be stressed enough: Just because something works for your friend (or racing foe), that doesn't mean it will work for you. You must experiment to discover what recovery methods actually work best for you.

Part Seven

SKILL BUILDING 201

Chapter 35

ADVANCED CLIMBING TECHNIQUES

It's one thing to grind your way up a steep climb, body rocking back and forth, bike barely moving forward—or even staying upright. It is another to gracefully ascend into the high mountains, your movements a lesson in fluidity, efficiency, and grace. Indeed, handling truly steep ascents (10 percent gradient or more) requires both fitness and skill. Here are some of the keys to progressing beyond survival mode when climbing.

Spin to win: Rather than grinding away in a larger gear, shift into an easier gear in order to keep your cadence high. Aim for at least 80 rpm, 90 if you can muster it. For most cyclists, this higher spin rate will lengthen the time before their legs become flushed with momentum-killing lactic acid.

Of course, one's ability to keep the legs churning will be influenced largely by the available gearing on your bike. It used to be that if you wanted to ditch the heavier triple chainring setup, your only alternative was a 53-39 double chainring, which frankly doesn't bode well for going up steeps hills. That 39-tooth little ring is too large for most amateur cyclists to spin up really steep hills. But nowadays many, if not most, bikes come stock with 52-36 mid-compact setups, or even 50-34 compact gearing. The smaller little ring allows you to spin that higher cadence. And while you do lose some top-end speed because of the smaller big ring, unless you're a wannabe sprinter this shouldn't be too big a deal.

Practice standing: When a climb becomes so steep that your cadence drops below 70 rpm, it is time to rise out of the saddle. This allows you to use your upper body to help your legs keep the pedals moving. In order to get comfortable and efficient with this position, use long, gentle hills to practice moving from a seated to standing position. Your seated position should be with hands on the bar tops near the stem. Pull lightly, keeping shoulders and hips square. This keeps your upper body relaxed to reduce energy cost and maximize lung capacity.

Before standing, switch your grip to the brake lever hoods. Rise and bring your hips forward, straightening and lengthening your lower back and opening your chest. The saddle's nose should just brush the back of your legs. Try not to pull with your arms on easy hills because it taxes your muscles with little return in speed. Let your weight help as you smoothly pull your body over one pedal, then over the other. Pull up on the right hood as you push down with your right foot, alternating right arm/right foot, left arm/left foot. The bike will rock subtly beneath you, establishing a rhythmic powering of the pedals.

Sit down when you can: Get out of the saddle as much as necessary to climb longer hills comfortably, but don't stay standing forever. For most riders, standing is more fatiguing because it uses extra upper-body muscle. Many riders alternate periods of sitting and standing just to mix up the stress on various muscle groups.

Keep quiet: Your upper body, that is. On steep grades, come up off the saddle and hold your bike as vertical as possible, with minimal sway. It's critical to keep your shoulders squared and facing forward. Don't drop them or create a snaking motion that wastes energy. In order to maintain momentum on a steep grade, you need to be rock-solid off the saddle. Many riders don't control their body and bike motion, making climbing a struggle. Work on being quiet and efficient.

Pull when necessary: If the grade threatens to rob your momentum completely and you are nearly at a standstill, try pulling back with both hands in unison on each downstroke. This lets you put maximum force into the pedals to keep the bike moving. Continue until the grade lessens and you can return to a normal climbing technique.

Eat at the base: Give your body a shot of fuel right before you start your big effort. It's a lot easier to slurp down a gel or take a bite of a bar when you are not completely cross-eyed.

Pace yourself: Rather than speeding up, slowing down, and speeding up again, try to find a pace that you can sustain for the entire climb. "It's easier to climb utilizing a constant rhythm than it is to surge and slow, which is more taxing on your body," says Scott Moninger, former pro racer turned coach.

Do hill repeats: One of the most common mistakes riders make at hill climb events is going too hard early in the effort and not saving any energy for the finish, says coach Trevor Connor. To avoid this, practice doing hill repeats in the 8- to 10-minute range where your effort is the same every time. "The idea is to teach pacing," says Connor. "The usual pattern is that the person pins it during the first one, then goes progressively slower. I strive to get people to do the efforts within 15 to 20 seconds of each other. This really helps you figure out what your fastest time up a climb would be without blowing up before the finish."

Train for the effort: If you know that an upcoming event has a 5-mile climb that averages 8 percent gradient, do your best to replicate that effort in training. Like anything else, practice begets improvement—and doing your best to replicate the climb in training will get your mind and body prepared for how the effort might feel during the event.

Get inspired: On the day of your race or big ride, tape some inspiring messages or photos to your top tube. "This will give you something to focus on besides the pain in your legs and lungs," says Jeremy Powers, multitime US national cyclocross champion.

Relax: It's hard to relax when your heart is beating out of your chest, your legs are throbbing, and your lungs are burning. But do your best. Keeping your muscles constantly flexed will quickly wear you down. Efficient climbing is a measured effort, where you only want to use the strength and energy necessary to keep your momentum. Gradually, you'll learn to maintain a controlled style while staying relaxed and breathing evenly. And don't fret if you can't always keep your proverbial cool. Hauling your bike up truly steep grades is tough no matter what you do.

Chapter 36

THE ART OF THE ROTATING PACELINE

Sharing the pace with others allows you to ride faster and with less effort. The keys are working together, building trust, and paying attention. At the elite level, pacelines become art forms. Riders move like a squadron of fighter pilots in a constantly flowing rhythm. Recreational riders may not be as graceful, but they can enjoy the benefits of riding in a paceline, too. In a century, riding in a group will allow you to finish faster and fresher. Busting a headwind isn't much fun alone, but with a few others to help, the miles pass quickly. Chapter 10 covered the basics of riding in a group. Now it's time to take it to the next level.

Rotating pacelines contain two lines of riders side by side, continuously in motion. This motion is achieved by one line going slightly faster than the other. Let's say that you're the lead rider in the faster line. You should cross over to the slow line after passing the front wheel of the rider beside you. Then you drift back with the others in the slow line. When the final position is reached at the back of the line, you drop in behind the back wheel of the last rider in the fast line (see tips to follow). When done right, this formation looks like a constantly rotating elliptical chain.

If you're confused, gather several friends and walk through the fundamentals in your living room. Try a single paceline first. Lead for 10 seconds, then pull off either to the right or left, then slide to the back of the line. Stay close enough to bump elbows, then move in behind the last person. Now try the double paceline. Form two lines, side by side. March up

When done properly a paceline is a thing of cycling beauty, allowing a group of riders to move faster together than they could alone.

the faster line, pull over to the front of the slower line, then drop back with it. Practice both clockwise and counterclockwise rotations.

Finally, go one step further and adjust for a crosswind. Wind direction determines which way to pull off. You always want to move into a crosswind. This way the advancing line, which is already working harder, gets some protection from the wind. In strong crosswinds riders become offset like geese on the wing. They also overlap wheels, which means a mistake can take down the whole bunch. The width of this type of paceline typically requires a completely traffic-free road.

By walking through the basics, you have already started to form some trust with your group. But before you try these skills on the road, here are 10 tips for becoming a master of the rotating paceline.

1. Put weaker riders behind stronger ones.

2. A paceline is a team. It's only as strong as its weakest member, so help that person out by both encouraging them and by not letting them get upset if they need to sit out a turn from time to time.

3. Start by riding slowly in low gears to get properly warmed up.

4. Get used to following closely to get the benefit of the draft. Skilled riders feel comfortable riding within inches of the wheel in front. In a rotating paceline, stay just as close side to side.

5. Ride smoothly and predictably. Never accelerate or brake quickly. If you are running up on the wheel in front, slow down (without braking) by moving into the wind slightly.

6. Maintain a constant speed when you get to the front by glancing at your cycling computer or GPS device. The tendency is to accelerate, but this will break the rhythm of the group.

7. If the rider at the front charges off, let that person go and hold your speed.

8. If you tire, sit out as many turns as necessary by staying at the back. Let riders coming back know that you are resting, and give them space to move in ahead of you.

9. As the speed increases, gaps may develop because riders can't hold the wheel ahead, or they miss the last wheel as they try to get back on the end of the paceline. Strong riders need to fill these gaps in order to preserve the flow, even if it means jumping across and moving back up the line early.

10. Though it's a natural instinct, don't focus on the wheel in front of you. This gives you little time to react to problems. Instead, keep your eyes up and scan about 30 feet ahead, looking through and past the riders in front of you.

Chapter 37

TRAINING THE BRAIN

To be a successful cyclist you need to set goals. Whether you are gearing up for a big ride or race, or if you just want to get over the next hill, goals are important. And perhaps more than anything, it's your ability to focus that helps you reach those goals.

Focus can be described as narrowing your attention. Focus is concentration. It lets you aim your vision and define your view. You choose a goal such as a gran fondo, century ride, or road race that you want to be in shape for, then commit to preparing for it. Staying focused on the goal and sustaining a strong mental image of the event will make it easier for you to put in the necessary work. Focus will help you get out the door for training rides that you may otherwise have skipped. Think of focus as the power of positive thinking taken to the next level.

"Positive thinking for the sake of positive thinking doesn't work all by itself," explains Julie Emmerman, PsyD, a clinical sport psychologist based in Boulder, Colorado, who has worked with dozens of professional and amateur cyclists, including a handful who have raced at the sport's highest level. "It doesn't work to just say I am great. It needs to be about recalling the training you have put into something, recalling why this is going to be a good experience. If you walk out of the house and everything is gloom and doom, you pick up on things and are skewed toward validating that inner experience. But if you have a positive attitude and mindset you will find things that reinforce that. So thinking that I am going to have a good ride today or I am going to have a great race automatically sets you up for seeking that which validates the thought."

Additionally, positive thinking is crucial because it helps you focus on the quality of your experience, not just the outcome. "Especially in bike racing you can't only think about the outcome or the results," continues Dr. Emmerman. "There is so much that can go wrong that's not in your control, so just to think about and focus on the outcome sabotages the experience."

Like focusing the lens of a camera, mental focus lets you see things more clearly so that you can concentrate on what is important. But you must develop this skill in order to zero in on the right elements. Concentrating on the long-term goal is good, but don't forget about the short-term goals that get you there.

Indeed, the steps up the ladder toward your goal should be savored and valued. Proper focus is putting blinders on, but not so tightly that you miss what's right in front of you. Visualizing your goal and the process required to reach it prepares you for the expected—and unexpected— turns in the road.

"I tell people to use imagery that draws on all senses," says Dr. Emmerman. "If someone is feeling anxiety about a race, I try to get them to conjure up all the senses of what they think the experience will be like. Picture yourself in the race, riding in a group, moving fast, and then ask do you feel like you can do that. Usually if the person has put the training in, then they start to see themselves doing well, and that reduces anxiety."

Dr. Emmerman views anxiety as a mass of energy, and we as humans (and cyclists) have a lot of control over how that mass is defined. If you do nothing, that mass can get out of control and cause panic. "But if you can use things like imagery, you can direct and form it so there is no room for free-floating anxiety. You have a plan," she says.

Short-term focus also means being able to clear your mind of everything extraneous so that you can concentrate on the task at hand. For instance, think about finishing the last 5 miles of the 60-mile training ride you're on instead of fretting about the chores you have to do when you get home. Indeed, successful short-term focus means thinking only about cycling at crucial moments. It allows you to be completely in the moment at that moment, and no place else.

Picture yourself riding in a group at a brisk pace, everyone close together. Imagine that some riders are struggling to keep a uniform speed and ride a straight line. This is no time to have your mind on the argument you just had with your spouse or to contemplate the latest crisis at work. In the most intense moments of cycling, the likelihood of making a mistake increases if you don't have complete focus. You may not even notice that your mind wanders at crucial times. On your next few rides, pay attention to how your mental state relates to various situations.

Studies have compared endurance athletes who zero in during races with those who zone out. Riders who zero in, who focus on the task at hand, which is called association, perform better. Disassociation, zoning out, is less productive because you take yourself out of the task rather than commit to it.

That doesn't mean you have to concentrate solely on cycling every minute of every ride. It's easy and natural to let your mind wander as you ride. In fact, it's often a healthy thing to do because cycling is such a good mental detox for stress. Let the warmup period of a ride be the time to clear your head. Then, once you're warm and ready, concentrate purely on the ride. The more concentrated your focus is, the more concentrated your enjoyment of the ride will be.

To train your concentration on specific aspects of cycling, do mental intervals. Focus on your breathing for 1 minute, then focus on your pedaling for 1 minute. As with any interval workout, rest between concentration periods.

Chapter 38

DEALING WITH FEAR

If while riding your bike you've ever crashed hard, had a run-in with a car, or even just a close call with a wayward deer, you likely know the feeling of fear. Whether you suffered significant bodily harm or not, the mental scars can linger, leaving you tentative, even nervous every time you head out for a spin. This is essentially a form of posttraumatic stress disorder, and it's a very real ailment that can suck the pleasure out of your two-wheeled fun.

But don't despair. There is a way past the anguish of trauma, assures Julie Emmerman, PsyD, a clinical sport psychologist based in Boulder, Colorado. Just like when you're trying to psyche yourself up for a race or long ride, Dr. Emmerman says positive thinking can also play a role in overcoming a traumatic experience such as a crash.

"Say you had an accident involving a car," she explains. "You need to think about how many times you have ridden your bike without incident versus how many times this one traumatic occurrence happened."

According to Dr. Emmerman, traumatic experiences get lodged in a part of your brain called the medulla, which is responsible for the fight-or-flight response. So even though your bad experience happened just once, it can get frozen in your mind. To promote the proverbial thaw you need to remind yourself of all the good times and dwell on those instead of dwelling on the bad.

"This helps diffuse the toxicity of that one experience in your mind," she continues. "This isn't just thinking positively in an airy-fairy way, but in a more constructive and rational way. You need to actively look for the things that are positive."

In another example, Dr. Emmerman talks about having a bad experience on a descent (perhaps a deer darted in front of you) and how to regain your downhill mojo.

"If you are really scared about descending a certain road, it doesn't work to just think positively and go," she says. "Instead try to focus on how you place your weight on your bike, and where your pedals go, and where your eyes look. You hear the wind and feel the temperature. All this helps take your attention away from the negative experience and the fear it's caused. Also try to be aware of the difference between being frozen in fear versus feeling relaxed and fluid."

It can also help to take a problematic section of road and break it into more manageable chunks. Instead of trying to ride the troublesome descent top-to-bottom all at once, do one section several times in a row until you begin to feel more comfortable on it.

"When people are really afraid, they lose their sense of internal awareness," adds Dr. Emmerman. "So it helps to simply ask yourself if the situation at hand really poses a threat, because in many case you'll realize there is not a real threat. It's just in your mind. The bottom line is that you need to control what you can control and then surrender to the rest. You can't spend your life worrying about every car on the road or you'll never be able to relax and ride."

Chapter 39

CROSS-TRAINING

For pro cyclists, cross-training during the racing season is typically taboo. It's all riding all the time. But being one-dimensional has its downsides, especially if you're not earning your living on the bike. Some cyclists become so specialized that a run through the airport to catch a plane can cause incredible muscle soreness.

Then there's the simple fact that doing the same thing all the time has a tendency to get boring. No one is telling you to stop riding your bike. But mixing a little variety into your life is good for both body and brain. You'll also likely see new opportunities unfold as you realize the fun that can be had running, hiking, swimming, skiing, or whatever other new activity you try. Remember that whole spice-of-life thing?

There are also some very distinct physiological benefits to cross-training. One major attribute of cross-training is the development of new aerobic and anaerobic pathways.

Think of your arterial system, which takes oxygen from your lungs and energy from various sources, as a series of small roads working in perfect harmony to move traffic. In order to be a good cyclist, you must refine the pathways to the muscle groups that are specific to cycling. This concept has long been the foundation of the argument for an athlete to be very sport specific. But a side effect of this specificity is that these pathways and muscle groups can become overworked and fatigued, because cyclists tend to work the same systems and muscle groups the same way, day after day, and complete recovery rarely occurs.

Enter cross-training. Cross-training can be rejuvenating and help rest those tired systems and muscle groups (not to mention a tired psyche).

Instead of slogging along day after day with dead legs, with cross-training you can still burn calories and get that all-important endorphin boost. When you climb on the bike the next day you will feel fresh and strong.

Look at your training plan and categorize what you do. Designate one category for cycling-specific training. Designate the other category for all other training. Training that is non-cycling-specific generally involves endurance-based activities, but without the same mechanics as riding. Think hiking, running, skiing, and so on.

Now evaluate those non-cycling options. What do you like to do? What's available where you live? Here are some suggestions, but don't be constrained just to activities on this list. If jazzercise is your thing, do it.

Running: It's hard to train your cardiovascular system on the bike if your legs are tired from too much riding. But because running uses different muscles, you can get aerobic benefit from it while giving your cycling muscles a break. Running is also great for anaerobic threshold work, because it requires you to carry your weight. When you are tight on time, running is a highly efficient way to use that time. And running doesn't require much equipment; all you have to do is lace up your shoes and go. Just make sure you ease into it. Fit cyclists who go for a hard run are usually easy to spot by their limp. When just starting out, use the run-walk method, running for 1 to 2 minutes, then walking for 2 to 3 minutes. As your body grows accustomed to the new activity, slowly ramp up your running intervals while decreasing your walk time. Treadmills or trail running are also good alternatives because they offer a softer surface, meaning there will be less impact on your joints.

Swimming: Time in the water allows you to maintain or improve certain aspects of your physiology with no impact on joints or muscles. Swimming tones and strengthens your upper body, giving balance to your physique. It is also great for developing a stronger torso and shoulders. Swimming stretches and elongates your leg muscles, which can relieve muscles that have been confined to the motion of pedaling. The downside is that you need a place to swim, which may require spending money on a health club membership.

Nordic skiing: Whether you opt for classic or skate skiing, this is one of the best aerobic activities there is because it involves both your upper and lower body. Indeed, it's well documented that elite level cross-country skiers are among the world's fittest athletes with the highest VO$_2$ max, a measure of the amount of oxygen one's body can take in and use each minute. Nordic skiing is also a great way to spend time outdoors, getting that all-important hit of vitamin D from the sun. Just remember to lather on sunscreen.

Cyclocross: Okay, this is just another form of riding your bike, albeit a really fun one. Cyclocross has its origins in road cycling: European road racers used it as a way to stay fit during their fall/winter offseason. But it's since become a popular amateur participation sport in North America. Places like Boulder, Colorado; Portland, Oregon; and the Boston, Massachusetts area play host to a large number of competitive events that feature hundreds of entrants. Cyclocross races are typically 45 minutes long, with participants navigating a circuit that includes some combination of dirt, grass, mud, sand, and pavement. The course typically features obstacles such as barriers or stairs that require you to dismount your bike, then quickly jump back on. Thus cyclocross is a great full-body workout because at varying times you are pedaling, running, and carrying your bike.

Mountain bike: Getting off the road and into the woods is another great way to mix things up. Yes, you'll still be spinning your legs, but mountain biking typically involves slower speeds and lower cadence, which will change the stress on your muscles. Your upper body will also get a workout as you push and pull on the handlebars while negotiating tricky terrain. Riding singletrack trails also requires the development of precise bike handling skills that will help make you a better overall cyclist.

Hit the gym: Whether you're into lifting weights, doing yoga, or taking a Pilates class, the local health club can be a great place to work out, especially when it's freezing outside. One great option is circuit training, where you combine a small variety of exercises into a single 5- to 10-minute session. For example, without any rest between exercises, you might do 15 to 20 lunges, 20 to 30 situps, 10 to 15 pushups, 15 to 20 bent-over rows. After a small break, you repeat the circuit two or three times. This type of training will not only yield gains of strength and tone, but will increase your heart rate, meaning you get some aerobic benefit, too.

Chapter 40

DRESSING FOR THE COLD

Summer may be the most fun time to ride, but winter is where cycling stories are born. No one remembers that one spin in the middle of summer when the sun was shining. But you'll likely never forget the time you braved the bitter elements, navigated a snow-packed road, and had a great time on your bike while less hearty souls were back home sitting in front of the TV.

The first rule of cold-weather riding is to dress in layers. Use fabrics with good moisture-transfer capability so that sweat can dissipate to the outside and leave your skin relatively dry. That means no cotton, which has poor wicking capacity. And skip standard wool, which insulates well but stays wet.

Instead opt for one of the many high performance, cold-weather-oriented fabrics that have flooded the cycling market in recent years. Manufacturers such as Pearl Izumi, Castelli, Gore, Specialized, Rapha, POC, and Pactimo all make a wide array of cycling clothing that's designed to keep the chill of old man winter at bay without overheating you, the rider.

The next rule is, when possible, do a little testing before committing to an outfit. Say you are headed out for a 2-hour ride with friends on a 32-degree day. Get dressed a little early so you can spend some time experimenting on a short loop around your house.

"Maybe you start out with a heavy long-sleeve jersey and a jacket," says Derrick Lewis, the North American retail and communications manager for cycling apparel maker Rapha, and who once commuted to work in Minneapolis for nearly an entire winter. "Take a 10-minute spin and if you don't feel a little chilly, circle back and dump a layer. The reason is that, once you are about 30 minutes into your ride, your heart will get going and your circulation will pick up and you'll start to get hot. Being hot means getting wet with sweat, and that can lead to you getting really cold."

Lewis's other key piece of advice is to stop obsessing over fingers and toes and instead think about your core. "Keeping your chest and shoulders warm is key," he explains. "Your body has a very clear self-defense mechanism. If your core temperature drops even half a degree, it contracts veins to your outer extremities because it knows it can lose a couple fingers and toes and still survive. But it can't let the core area get too cold because that is where all the vital organs are."

That's why you always want to start your dressing routine with a base layer, which helps to keep your core warm and promotes the transmission of sweat away from your body. So for instance, on a 32-degree day, Lewis says he starts with a long-sleeve base layer and then a winter-weight long-sleeve jersey that has some wind-proofing on the chest area. Finally, he adds a light wind jacket or vest.

"That way, if I start to warm up I can take that light wind layer off and stuff it into a jersey pocket," adds Lewis. Indeed, it's a good idea to keep your last layer packable so that you can adjust on the fly once you are out on the road.

Below the waist, the same strategy applies. Consider wearing a pair of thermal bib shorts with a pair of lighter-weight winter tights over them. This will keep your core area warm but let your legs breathe a little more since they are the ones doing all the work. Just don't let your knees get too cold.

Jeremy Powers also knows a little something about riding in the cold. The multitime US national cyclocross champion has long earned a paycheck battling foes—and Mother Nature—during this cycling discipline that takes place in fall and early winter. Whether competing on the European cross circuit, racing in the United States, or training at home in Massachusetts, Powers is constantly looking for the right balance between staying warm and staying comfortable and dry.

In general he says he looks for apparel that can adjust to a varying temperature range. That typically means lots of zippers, which allow him to open and close ventilation as the mercury and his internal temperature rise and fall. One of Powers's go-to pieces is a softshell jacket with zippers at the chest and underneath the armpits. Powers also loves neck warmers because they keep heat from escaping out the opening of a jersey or jacket. "If your core is warm, you'll be warm," he says, echoing Lewis.

Gloves are another key consideration for Powers. He often opts to bring two pairs. "That way if you start to get sweaty, you can swap on the new dry pair," he explains. "Otherwise the wind starts hitting that perspiration, which translates to you getting cold hands. And nothing ruins a ride quicker than not being able to feel the brake levers."

While it's hard to shift gears or use the brakes with full-on mittens, split-finger gloves are a good option on really cold days. These have one compartment for your thumb, one for your first two fingers, and a third for your ring and pinkie fingers. This design pools heat almost as well as mittens, but allows you to maintain some semblance of manual dexterity.

Further down, Powers focuses on his knees, usually opting for a pair of thermal tights that have some wind protection at the knee. "Your knees are doing a lot of work when you are riding," he says. "You want to keep them warm so everything in there stays nice and lubricated."

This falls in line with one of cycling's oldest traditions, which says anytime the temperature is below 65 degrees, your knees should be covered. A set of lightweight knee warmers will suffice until the temperature gets below 50 degrees or so.

As part of his multilayer approach, Powers employs a trick to protect his feet. First he puts on winter-weight socks, then his cycling shoes, and then he slips a thermal hand-warmer packet (think skiing) onto the top of his shoe and secures it in place with a cotton shoe cover. For the last layer, he puts on a pair of neoprene booties, which keep road spray at bay.

Powers also gives a general nod to merino wool. It is the super-material of the wool family because of its ability to breathe and insulate so well. This soft, lightweight fabric is used in socks, base layers, and even some cycling jerseys. "It does a great job of wicking and keeping heat in," he says.

"It sounds a little crazy, but I keep notes for all these different layering combinations based on the temperature," Powers adds. "That helps me take a lot of the guesswork out and I just focus on getting out for my ride."

But before heading out for that ride, Powers always gives his bike a good once-over. Fixing a punctured tire or other basic mechanical issue is a minor inconvenience in summer but a potential disaster in dead of winter. Even 5 minutes of standing around can give you a severe chill that you can't shake.

Chapter 41

RIDING IN THE RAIN

Does riding on wet, slippery surfaces make you nervous and twitchy? Do you hide inside when Mother Nature lets loose? While a measured amount of caution is always a good idea on slick roads, there's no reason to let a little precipitation prevent you from riding your bike. Instead, toss on some rain gear and heed these 12 tips for riding safely in the rain.

Practice: Practice may not make perfect, but it will make you better. Rain or shine, view every corner on every ride as an opportunity to practice your cornering technique. The better you understand the mechanics of cornering and the more you are able to apply them, the more comfortable you will be in any situation—wet or dry. As you approach a turn, choose a line that allows you to carve a smooth arc through the turn. Start wide, cut to the apex, then swing wide again. At the same time shift your weight to the rear of the saddle, put the outside pedal down and press your foot to weight it, then lean the bike into the turn with gentle pressure on the inside of the handlebar. If this is all new to you, first practice on a grass field, then graduate to a traffic-free parking lot, and finally head out on the open road.

Squeegee your rims: If your bike is equipped with traditional rim brakes, understand that water reduces your brake pads' friction on the rims, which in turn compromises braking efficiency. To combat this, apply the brakes to both wheels well before you need to slow or stop so that the moisture is squeegeed away. As this happens, you may feel a subtle amount of grabbing, so be ready to loosen your grip or your wheels could lock up, causing you to skid.

Caution wet paint: Avoid riding on lane lines and other painted road markers. When wet, they can become much more slippery than unpainted blacktop because the paint fills in the pavement's traction-enhancing irregularities. When heading into a turn, plan your line so that you don't have to lean the bike much—if at all—on any painted surface.

Metal mania: The same axiom applies to wet metal objects, such as manhole covers and sewer grates. They are often even slicker than wet painted lines. Avoid them by looking ahead and carefully picking an alternative line. This is especially true for metal bridge surfaces and railroad tracks. Rain can make them slick as ice. Often the smart choice is to dismount and walk.

Don't fall in fall: Wet leaves are another potentially slippery surface, so take caution when riding on a rainy autumn day.

No puddle jumping: Try to avoid riding through puddles if you can't see the bottom of them. There could be a pothole or another ride-wrecking obstacle lurking underneath the water's murky surface.

See clearly: You can't ride if you can't see, so wear eye glasses to keep rain and road spray out of your eyes. Avoid dark tinted lenses and instead opt for clear or yellow lenses that help magnify road details even on the gloomiest of days.

Be seen: Rain reduces motorists' vision, so help them see you by dressing in bright colors. Never wear a dull-hued rain jacket. It can act like camouflage on a gloomy day. Instead, choose wet-weather apparel that is bright yellow, orange, or red and that has reflective accents or piping.

Light up the night: You wouldn't drive your car in rain or low light without turning its lights on. You shouldn't ride your bike in these situations without lights, either. At minimum, affix a white headlight and red tail light to your bike. There are many affordable options on the market. Lights that have various modes, including flashing or burst, are a great option.

Be gentle: Don't dive into wet corners with reckless abandon. When turning, cautiously lean your bike. If leaned, your bike will turn. How much you need to lean depends on the turn's tightness, your speed, and the available traction. Wet roads don't automatically mean less traction, but assume they do until you know for sure otherwise. On slick turns, don't push the bike over too far because you may slide out. Maintain an even angle with both your bike and body by leaning gently over together. This lets the bike turn on its own instead of forcing it to turn.

Light touch: Brake evenly between the front and rear wheel. This helps you stay in control and keep the tires firmly planted on the road. Ease off the brakes as you enter a turn. (If necessary, you can continue to feather the rear brake.) Imagine that you're a stream of water plotting a smooth path around the corner. Flow like a river so that there is no jerky motion, only a seamless arc. Pick a smooth, gradual line so that motion is subtle and all reactions are soft.

Stay calm: Like so many things in life, remaining calm will help your cause. Think of driving a car. In poor conditions, a death grip on the wheel just ramps up your stress level and increases the likelihood that you end up in a ditch. The same is true on a bike. Tension magnifies mistakes. When approaching a turn or other typically nerve-wracking situation, take a few deep breaths, let your shoulders drop, slightly loosen your grip, and consciously let tension flow out of your body. You will be amazed at how much easier things become, no matter how hard it's raining.

Chapter 42

TIPS FOR RIDING DURING THE WINTER

Now that you know how to dress for riding in cold conditions, here are some tips to ensure that your winter rides are safe, comfortable, and productive.

Ride with a friend or group: Sharing conversation as well as a draft helps the miles go by. But unless you have some sort of early season goal, skip the hard, fast group rides during the winter months. Instead, use the winter season to accumulate base miles. Ride with others who also want to build base fitness.

Head into the wind to start each ride: Get it out of the way early when you're still fresh. If you work up a sweat, having a tailwind on the return trip will decrease the chill, while a headwind will make it worse.

Don't overdress: As stressed in the Chapter 40, if you're not chilly in the first few minutes of your ride, then you are probably overdressed and you may overheat later on.

Heat your liquids: If you're heading out on a subfreezing day, fill your water bottles with hot drinks such as herbal tea, and use insulated bottles if available. This will lengthen the time before your liquids turn to icy slush, increasing the chance you actually hydrate on your ride.

Watch out: Be wary of shaded corners, which may hide icy road surfaces.

Lighten up: Wear light, bright colors to help motorists see you on low light days. Bonus points for wearing clothing with reflective elements, which are common in performance wear these days.

Illuminate: Even when riding during daylight, attach lights to the front and rear of your bike. Just a small flashing blinky might mean the difference between being seen and seeing the inside of an ambulance.

Be prepared: Carry two tubes instead of the usual one. Dealing with a puncture on a cold day is no fun. Patching a tube with freezing fingers is miserable.

Keep going: Don't stop for long, if at all. You want to keep your core temperature up, so putzing around on the side of the road could lead to shivers you'll never shake.

Don't overdo it: As a general rule, you can be fairly comfortable for 90 minutes in subfreezing temperatures. But things may deteriorate quickly after that, particularly if you have been sweating.

Break it up: Don't be afraid to break up your ride. If your goal is 4 hours for the day, consider splitting that up into a pair of 2-hour rides, and throw in a recovery nap if you have the time.

Take time to recover: Winter takes more out of you. Because of the elements and your lower fitness level, a 50-mile winter ride could feel like 80 miles would in the middle of the summer.

Take a break: Even if you live somewhere where winters are mild and you can comfortably ride all year long, you still need to take a little time off. Use winter for recovery so you don't get caught in the flying-in-January, dead-by-June trap.

Part Eight

RACING AND RIDING FAST

Chapter 43

GET AERO, GO FASTER

Initially you might question the importance of aerodynamics in road cycling. Relatively speaking, you're not moving all that fast. How much could it really matter? Well, just ask Greg LeMond. Coming into the final stage time trial of the 1989 Tour de France, LeMond was looking up at what seemed an insurmountable 50-second deficit to Frenchman Laurent Fignon. Most thought the race for the final yellow jersey was over. French newspapers had already started printing special editions honoring Fignon's feat.

Fignon rode a time trial bike with front and rear disc wheels and bullhorn-style handlebars. His position on the bike was otherwise very much like he was out riding a normal road race. By contrast, LeMond sought every possible aerodynamic advantage. The American wore an aero helmet, used a rear disc wheel, and mounted a pair of aero handlebars on the front of his bike. Unlike Fignon, LeMond's hands, elbows, and head were tucked down into the now-familiar time trial position.

By the end of the day, LeMond secured the overall title by 8 seconds, in what remains the closest finish in the Tour's storied history. Of course, fitness and ability played a huge role in the outcome. LeMond had been riding well throughout the race, but clearly the equipment and on-the-bike positioning choices he made created a significant difference. From then on, cyclists and manufacturers of bicycles, gear, and apparel have been seeking ways to improve aerodynamic efficiency.

This quest to shave seconds by reducing drag typically starts in a wind tunnel, where it is possible to measure the effects of changes in body position and equipment. The lower your drag, the faster you will travel without any change to expended effort. It is literally free speed.

Gear such as an aero helmet, disc wheels, and a time trial bike
can all conspire to make you faster.

Specialized is among the host of bike manufacturers that puts massive research and development resources into finding ways to increase aerodynamic efficiency. In 2013, the company took the heretofore unprecedented step of building its own wind tunnel facility at its Morgan Hill, California, world headquarters. Since then, Specialized's team of engineers have spent countless hours doing wind tunnel testing, examining everything from the effects of frame tube shapes to assessing the difference between shaved and hairy legs. (Shaved is faster.)

"The number-one thing is the position of the rider because they are responsible for so much of the overall drag, 70 to 80 percent depending on the person's size," explained Specialized R&D engineer and aerodynamic expert Chris Yu. "At the same time you need a position you can maintain. If you have to sit up all the time because your back is hurting you, then that super-low position isn't doing you a whole lot of good."

Here are Yu's top tips on how to increase your aerodynamic efficiency to get faster on your bike.

Dress fast: While most cyclists think bike frames and wheels have the most significant impact on aero efficiency, Yu says the best bang for your buck is clothing. "Take that day-glow windbreaker you see so many people wearing at the start of a century ride because it is a little chilly in the morning," said Yu. "Well a lot of people won't stop to take it off simply because they don't want to lose that time. So when they start to get hot during the second half of the ride, they will just unzip and let it flap in the wind for the last 50 miles. Well, we did a simulation like that and found that roughly it will cost you 10 to 15 minutes over that span if your jacket is flapping in the wind the whole time. So you would be much better off stopping to take it off, having a snack, and doing some stretching." Better yet, Yu advises riders to wear tight-fitting clothing such as arm warmers and a thermal jersey. "You will stay warm—and be faster," he added.

Lower can be slower: For years, the traditional view of the on-bike position was that the lower you got, the faster you would be. But Yu says all riders eventually hit a point of diminishing return. "There inevitably comes a point where the amount of power you can put out starts to drop," he said of seeking a super-low position. "And you have to be able to maintain that position, so if you are sitting up to stretch every 15 minutes that is slowing you down." For this reason, Yu recommends getting a professional bike fit, which can help you find that ideal position that splits the difference between fast, efficient, and maintainable.

If a bike fit isn't in the budget right now, try this instead. On a long hill with a steady grade, time yourself coasting downhill in various positions. Then, check your power output by riding your bike on a stationary trainer, using progressively larger gears and comparing them with your heart rate. The bigger the gear that you can use for a given heart rate, the greater your power. Once you know the position where you are most aero, and the effort level where you are most powerful, find a middle ground that translates to the greatest speed on the road.

Lower your frontal area: One easy trick you can do at home, says Yu, is to get set up on an indoor trainer and then look at your on-bike position in the mirror. "The goal is to reduce your frontal area," said Yu. "So maybe it's tucking your elbows in, or getting your knees to track straight up and down instead of bowing out. Look at how your body is positioned and how you are moving on the bike, then try to make changes that will lower your overall frontal area. Then go out and test those positions on the road to see if you can comfortably maintain them." If you can't, don't immediately just give up. Try increasing your flexibility through stretching or yoga.

Shave your legs: While most men new to cycling wince at the idea of shaving their legs, Yu says this oldest of cycling traditions has legitimate benefits beyond simply fitting in. "We've tested a number of different riders and the average time saved is about 50 seconds over 40 kilometers," revealed Yu. "So you will be faster and adhering to the traditions of cycling."

Clean up your bike: We're not talking soap and water (though a clean bike typically works better and lasts longer). Instead Yu points at items such as oversized saddlebags and unkempt cables and housing. "It is all unnecessary drag that is slowing you down," he said. "If you don't need that extra 10 centimeters of cable housing, trim it."

Frame shapes count: Though it's hard to specify exact gains because of the near limitless differences in rider size and speed, Yu says your bike's frame is the piece of equipment that has the largest effect on aerodynamic drag. That is followed in order by clothing, helmet, and wheels. "In one baseline test we developed in our wind tunnel, the frame was worth about a minute of time savings over a 40 kilometers time trial, with apparel next at 45 seconds," said Yu. "A helmet with an improved aero shape netted a 42-second gain, and wheels were about 30 seconds, though that was into a headwind. Wheels will be more important in a crosswind situation."

Chapter 44

MASTERING THE ART OF THE SPRINT

For many fans of professional bike racing, mass field sprints are the most exciting part of the sport. After hours of racing, the day's outcome comes down to one final mad dash to the finish line. But before the true sprinters come to the fore, there is a carefully orchestrated plan where teammates take turns at the front, keeping the speed high and keeping their designated sprint leader out of the wind until that final moment. It's called a leadout train. In this regard, road cycling is somewhat like football, where blockers pave the way for the running back. Of course the speed—and consequences—are much higher in cycling. Nothing is quite as dramatic as a crash during a bunch sprint.

But why bother honing your sprint if you are not a competitive rider? What good is speed if your primary cycling goals are fitness and fun? For starters, sprinting is fun. Like a child running from friends in a game of tag, this is cycling's version of the high-speed getaway.

It's also a great way to add some competitive entertainment to your weekly group ride with friends. After a few hours of conversational-pace spinning, why not ramp up the speed and sprint for the town limits sign? The winner gets bragging rights until next week.

Sprinting can also be helpful in emergency situations. Sprint away from that angry dog that bolts into the road, or sprint to avoid the car that doesn't quite make the yellow light and barrels through the intersection . . . headed straight at you. A quick burst of speed can save your life. And for many riders, cycling is a numbers game. We like to test our limits. How fast can you go? How many watts can you put out? Finally, sprinting is a great way to increase overall fitness. By training your muscles and cardiovascular system to perform during high-speed, high-output efforts, you will become a better all-around rider.

Train for Speed

Becoming a great sprinter requires special training. Try these workouts to improve your fitness and skills.

Spin sprints: Use gravity to improve your seated-sprinting form. Spin downhill at 120 to 150 revolutions per minute, choosing a gear that enables you to keep tension on the chain for 10 seconds or so. Repeat three to eight times. Concentrate on staying relaxed and pedaling in circles. If you bounce wildly on the saddle, use a slightly bigger gear. Low-gear accelerations are the best way to improve your pedal stroke and build leg speed.

Short sprints: Pick a road sign or telephone pole about 100 yards away. Jump out of the saddle in a lower gear. After this initial burst, you can opt to sit or remain standing, depending on your style, until you cross that imaginary line. Try 5 to 10 repetitions with full recovery between each effort. This drill helps build explosive power and leg speed.

Progressive shifting: Roll along easily on a flat road, then quickly ramp up your speed. Shift every 50 to 100 yards as you begin to spin out of your current gear. Aim for two to three shifts without losing any speed. This will typically take about 30 seconds. Do this drill two to four times during a workout to build sprint endurance as well as to dial in your shifting technique.

Hill sprints: Find a gradual hill that is 200 to 400 yards long. Roll about halfway up, then shift into the big chainring and sprint up to and over the summit. Try 2 to 5 reps with complete recovery between efforts. It is essential to maintain good form. This sprint will do wonders for your strength. Note that you'll need a solid base of fitness to successfully do this drill.

Here are some basic sprinting techniques to help you win your next mad dash to the finish line.

Go bigger: To set up for a sprint, choose a slightly larger gear than the one you can roll along in while comfortably spinning. Next, grasp your handlebars firmly in the drops.

Stand up: Start your sprint by coming off the saddle as your pedal goes past the 12 o'clock position. It doesn't matter which foot you start with. But if you kick a ball with your right foot, you will probably feel more natural using that one.

Go all in: Commit everything to the effort. Pull strongly with the arm that is on the same side as the pushing foot, counteracting your leg's downward force. But keep both arms fairly rigid so that the bike stays upright under you.

Stay back: Initially keep your weight back so that the rear wheel gets good traction during the early, high-torque phase of your sprint. Hold your body square to the bike. Let your hips and shoulders work in unison just like when you are climbing a hill out of the saddle.

Stay low: As you pick up speed, relax. Alternately pull and release the bar in sync with your downstrokes. Slowly rotate forward, keeping your body fairly low for better aerodynamics. Don't let your legs straighten completely at the bottom of each stroke. You want constant, fluid power going to the pedals. Also keep your head as low as you can while still keeping your eyes up—you need to see where you are going.

Chapter 45

REST MAKES YOU STRONGER

In Part Six, we detailed the keys of post-ride recovery nutrition. Recall that you must address your body's nutritional needs within the 30-minute post-ride window or suffer the consequences. Just as important (if not more) is the recovery time you give your body between training rides and races. Any coach will tell you that rest is what makes you stronger, because it is rest that allows your body to adapt to stress and be ready for the next hard workout or event.

"The whole idea of training is to place stress on your body, pushing it beyond what it can normally handle," says coach Trevor Connor. "Your body reacts by saying, 'I don't want to feel like that again, so I'm going to rebuild and get stronger.' It's what's known as super compensation, where your body recovers above the original baseline."

But this compensation doesn't happen if you don't recover properly. Indeed, one of the hardest skills to acquire as a cyclist is recognizing and addressing the signs of burnout, says Connor.

"So many people have this remarkable ability to see all the signs of being overly fatigued and still think they are fine," he explains. "They'll get scared, thinking this wasn't part of the plan, and just ignore it because they think if they take time off they are going to detrain and not be as strong. The reality is, that to achieve a physiological adaptation you have to tax your system by training but also give it time to recover properly."

Here are some tips for proper recovery—and for recognizing the signs that you may be overly fatigued.

Work doesn't equal recovery: One of the biggest differences between pro racers and the rest of us is that after a hard training ride they get to go home and put their feet up and relax. Most of the rest of us have to go back to our day jobs. "A lot of people think that sitting at their desk or on an airplane is a recovery day, but it's just not true," says Scott Moninger, former pro racer turned coach. "Real recovery is not riding your bike—and not stressing out over traveling or being at work answering a thousand e-mails." One great approach to recovery is to reallocate the time you would normally spend on the bike and use it to take a nap or stretch.

Get adequate sleep: How much sleep is enough sleep? There is no right answer. We've all heard the stories of CEOs who can run a company on a few hours of rest a night. But generally speaking somewhere between 7 and 9 hours of sleep per night should be the goal, according to the National Sleep Foundation. During periods of heavy exercise that number may increase, though. "The golden rule I use with people I coach is that if you have to set an alarm and are dragging yourself out of bed, then you are probably not getting enough sleep," says Connor. "But if you are getting seven hours a night and waking up on your own, then it's probably plenty. If you're not sure, get to bed early. If you end up waking up early on your own, then you'll have a few extra hours to yourself in the morning."

Track resting heart rate: First you need to know what your normal resting heart rate is. This measure should be taken first thing in the morning when you are not feeling fatigued. Once you know that number, pay attention to any instance when you are four or five beats a minute or more above normal. When that happens it's a sign of fatigue, meaning you should back off your training load until things return to normal. "For me that usually means my recovery is commensurate to current training stress," says Connor. "So if I did a hard five-day training camp, afterward I would take two or three days off the bike, then do another few days of easy spinning. Basically, the deeper you go with your training, the more intense your recovery needs to be."

Track heart rate during rides: Another sure sign of fatigue is a lagging heart rate. If you are going at a pace that would normally push your heart rate to 140 or 150 beats a minute, but you can barely break 120, take heed. "That is when it's time to turn around and get some rest," advises Connor.

Try active recovery: Recovery rides are a great way to promote healing. The idea of active recovery, says Connor, is that you get your blood flowing without taxing your muscles. "After a really hard training day or race, you'll have a whole bunch of inflammation localized around the muscles, and those muscles are trying to rebuild," he explains. "So the two things that need to happen are to clear out the inflammation and get the nutrients to the muscles in the form of amino acids and carbs so they can rebuild and restock fuel sources. If you can get some blood flow to that area, you can speed up that process. The trick is that a lot of people have a hard time going easy on their easy days. The reality is that you should be in your small chainring unless you are going downhill with a tailwind. Sixty-year-olds on commuter bikes should be passing you."

Chapter 46

THE CADENCE QUESTION

Check out race videos from the Tour de France in the early 2000s and you will notice one very distinct difference between the two main combatants for the yellow jersey.

On the ever-important climbing stages, German Jan Ullrich grinds away, pushing bigger gears at a lower cadence. (He was known as a masher.) Meanwhile, Lance Armstrong's legs are a whirr of motion as he spins a lower gear at a faster rate of speed. (Lance was the quintessential spinner.)

Now forget for a second all the dark history these two riders conjure up. Focus instead on what the image of these two different pedaling styles reveals about choosing the right cadence when riding your bike. Are you a big-gear grinder? Are you a small-gear spinner? Something between these two extremes? The reality is that there is no one-size-fits-all cadence. Indeed, you will benefit from different cadences for different types of efforts, say climbing a steep hill versus barreling along on the flats.

"There is a lot of research out there but nothing that is absolutely definite that supports one style over the other in all cases," reveals coach Trevor Connor. "Some studies have found that 60 to 70 rpm was ideal because it used less oxygen than spinning in the 90 to 100 rpm range. But then subsequent research revealed that as power output increases, a higher cadence was better."

So on one hand, pedaling a higher cadence, say 80 to 90 rpms, can be more efficient because it is less taxing on your muscles. But if you get bogged down from that high cadence, and you don't feel comfortable churning along at a lower cadence, you will be in trouble. Having the ability to turn over the pedals at a lower cadence, say when a climb gets truly steep, is a good skill to have.

It's for this reason that Connor implores the riders he works with to be as well-rounded as possible. "If the person's knees can handle it, I like to have them do some big-gear climbing work mixed with higher cadence efforts," he explains. "One workout I have people do is 20 minutes at a lower cadence, around 50 to 60 rpm, and then some shorter 8- to 10-minute repeats in the 80 to 90 rpm range."

To understand the difference in these two efforts, think of a basic barbell curl. First pick up a 10-pound weight and curl it three times. Now pick up a 30-pound weight and repeat the same motion just once.

"Lifting the 10-pound weight isn't going to be particularly fatiguing," adds Connor. "But even just one curl of the 30-pound weight might be more than you can handle. Now translate that to cycling and you can see why you don't want to be totally incapable of one or the other, because being able to comfortably push both low and high cadence will come in handy at some point."

As this example illustrates, pushing a bigger gear at a lower cadence requires strength. "You will be recruiting more muscle fiber, which in turn will make you fatigue faster. Whereas if you keep a high cadence you are using less muscle fiber, and thus will stay fresher longer. Plus if you are always spinning at a low rpm, it's hard to adjust up in a race when someone attacks," says Conner.

There's also an argument that the type of effort should influence the cadence you choose.

"I had a different cadence depending on what I was doing," says Scott Moninger, former pro racer turned coach. "If I was doing an eight-corner criterium, I usually felt more comfortable pushing a higher cadence. But for time trial efforts, I liked to push a heavier gear with a slower rpm."

Moninger also claims his fitness level would influence the cadence he chose when racing. "If I was feeling really good, I might run a higher cadence to spin the lactic acid out," he says. "But if I was struggling or having a yo-yo kind of day, I'd go to bigger gear because I could sometimes drop my heart rate that way, even if it would cause the legs to load up a little more."

Jeremy Powers, a multitime US national cyclocross champion, says that he typically defers to a higher cadence when racing on the road. "I'm always in the 90 to 100 rpm range, but you also see plenty of guys, especially the bigger, stronger guys, who are pushing a lower cadence," says Powers. "But for me higher was always easier on the body. Pushing big gears can be really hard on your knees, especially if your on-bike position is off at all."

Bottom line: Don't be afraid to experiment with different cadences for different situations to find out what works best for you. At the end of the day, the best cadence is that one that produces your best performance.

Chapter 47
DEALING WITH KNEE PAIN

Ugly medical terms are associated with knees and bikes, words that sound like trouble when you say them. Chondromalacia, patellar tendinitis, medial synovial plica syndrome, iliotibial band syndrome—a medical rogues' gallery of pain and misery.

Does this mean that bike riding is hard on knees? Far from it. In fact, when these injuries are mentioned, cycling is often the rehabilitation of choice. Physical therapists know that when you can't run, walk, or hobble, you can often pedal.

"Injured or surgically repaired knees want movement, and you want movement," says Andrew Pruitt, EdD, founder of Colorado's highly regarded Boulder Center for Sports Medicine, now the CU Sports Medicine and Performance Center. "These things come together on the bike."

Still, knee injuries are an occasional fact of the cycling life, simply because of the number of revolutions a rider makes. At an average cadence of 90 revolutions per minute, a rider cranks out 5,400 strokes each hour, or about 1.5 million in a 5,000-mile year. That's a lot of potential wear and tear on cartilage, ligaments, and tendons.

Repetition isn't the only villain. The knee is anything but a simple joint that pumps up and down in a linear, piston-like motion. Instead, Dr. Pruitt says, the knee rolls, glides, and rotates in several planes during each pedal stroke. The cycling leg is anchored at the bottom by the foot, which is attached to the pedal with a rigid shoe. At the other end is the massive bone and ligament edifice of the hip joint. The knee moves between these fixed

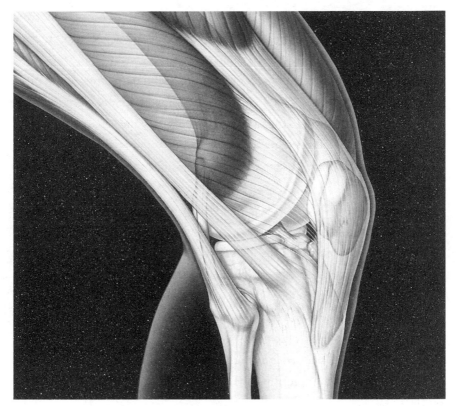

Proper on-bike position goes a long way to preventing knee pain.

points, and if this isn't accommodated by correct body position on the bike and proper placement of the foot on the pedal, bad things happen.

How do you safeguard your knees so that 10 to 20 million pedal strokes down the road they will still be going strong? The key is knowing what to do and what to avoid—on the bike or off.

First, perfect your position. Problems aren't limited to neophytes. Even experienced riders make mistakes when setting up a new bike. Among the best bike fitting methods is dynamic fit, which means the rider is fit on their bike while pedaling rather than when sitting stationary, and that fit is then assessed via video analysis.

Static measurements can also approximate your ideal position. For saddle height, one popular method was developed in the 1980s. Stand shoeless with your feet shoulder-width apart and have someone measure your inseam from the floor to your crotch. Multiply the result by 0.883. That number is your seat height from the top of the saddle to the middle of the bottom bracket axle measured along the seat tube. This number is only a starting point, so fine-tune it based on experience.

For instance, riders with long feet and those who pedal toes down often require a higher saddle height. A saddle that's too high may cause pain in the back of the knee, while one that's too low usually produces pain in the front of the knee. Saddle setback, or fore/aft position, is best adjusted with the bike on a stationary trainer. See Chapter 2 for details on how to adjust your riding position.

Of course, what you do on your bike will also go a long way to promoting or alleviating knee pain. Here are some tips to assure it's the latter.

Keep your knees toasty: Riding in 40°F with red, chapped knees is a recipe for trouble. Pros routinely cover their legs in training when the temperature is below 60°F. While each individual's tolerance will differ, there's certainly no harm in keeping muscles and joints warm.

Warm up: Just as with most sports, a little warmup time to get blood flowing and muscles primed is a good idea. As a general rule, aim for at least 15 minutes of moderate spinning before you attack the local climb or go hard on the flats.

Spin: Look at video of the pros in action and you'll notice their rapid and fluid pedal strokes. Try this drill to improve your pedal stroke: The next time you are going up your favorite climb, use a gear at least two teeth lower (thus easier) than usual. This higher cadence is easier on your joints.

Build mileage gradually: Your first ride after the winter offseason shouldn't be 5 hours long. Instead, start with a lower mileage and build slowly, increasing your total mileage no more than 10 percent per week.

Beware of change: Your body likes consistency, so when you alter equipment, your knees often protest. Whether you get a new bike, new shoes, new pedals, or change stem length, go easy at first to give yourself time to adapt.

Get fit: If knee pain persists, consider getting a professional bike fit. It could end up being the best money you ever spent on your cycling habit.

Chapter 48

INVESTIGATION OF OVERTRAINING

Cycling, it's often said, is a sport for tough guys. And tough guys don't get tired. Fatigue is a phenomenon of the mind, not the legs. Ride more to get stronger.

Ann Snyder, PhD, an exercise physiology professor at the University of Wisconsin–Milwaukee met a bunch of these tough guys and decided to find out how tough they really were. For 2 weeks, Dr. Snyder subjected them to more than 10 hours of interval training per week, plus races on weekends. One rider couldn't sustain the load, dropping from the study after 6 days. Seven others survived. By the end, only one was able to finish a race.

The findings? Bike riders are indeed tough. "Cyclists are crazy," says Dr. Snyder with a mixture of awe and fascination. "You can get them to do anything."

Aside from this simple summation, her study produced a number of concrete findings. All of the subjects displayed a downturn in performance, as indicated by their time trial and power output tests. Sleeping heart rate increased, while maximum heart rate declined. Also, subjective responses to a questionnaire showed a deterioration in their "general state of well-being."

But most interesting, Snyder followed the 2 weeks of intense training with a 2-week rest period in which the training load was roughly halved. Here, performance reached its former level or improved. This points out one of the central dilemmas of training: We know that hard work makes us faster, but how much is too much? And how long does it take to recover and experience this rebound effect?

Exercise physiologists are fond of making a distinction between over-training, which is debilitating and long-term (lasting weeks or months), and overreaching, which is what we feel at the end of a particularly hard week of riding. With adequate recovery, overreaching will make us faster and stronger. Overtraining, by contrast, is a road to ruin. Unfortunately, the border between these two conditions is vague. And either way, it's a dangerous line to be on.

Dr. Snyder found this out in no uncertain terms while conducting her research. Although a few of her hardy bunch improved under the intense regimen, all showed physiological danger signs. In fact, for anyone who considers overtraining to be a figment of the imagination, the study debunked that concept with a fusillade of data. Of all Dr. Snyder's measurements, the only ones that didn't change were weight and body fat percentage. Other measures, however, revealed the dramatic effects of too much training.

VO_2 max: This measure of the body's ability to deliver oxygen to working muscles declined significantly, reaching its lowest point at the end of the intense 2-week training period.

Sleeping heart rate: Increased about five beats per minute after the period of hard training.

Maximum heart rate: Declined about seven beats per minute. In a race this could translate to poor performance.

Subjective evaluation: Riders were asked such questions as, "Would you like to skip training?" or "Do you feel as if you're not recovered?" Not surprisingly, there was a distinct lack of enthusiasm during the study. The moping was most pronounced the week after the intense training, during the rest period.

Time trials: Riders raced an 8.5-kilometer course once per week during the intense training period. Performance slowed significantly, an average of 41 seconds in the week after intense training. Also, riders could not attain the same heart rate that they did in the first time trial when they were fresh.

Maximum power output: Cyclists performed a weekly power test in which the load increased by 50 watts every 5 minutes until exhaustion. The result? Power output declined an average of 26 watts after the intensive training.

Despite the obvious risks, let's say that you decide to embark on a similar period of intense training (or overreaching). How long must you rest before you can reap the benefits? Dr. Snyder's study supplied some answers here, too.

The two key performance variables (time trials and maximum power output) continued to improve throughout the 2-week recovery period. Although the study ended after 2 weeks of recovery, the findings suggest that performance may have continued to improve with even more rest. In other words, the typical 2 days of tapering before an important event may not be enough.

Who is prone to these dangers? Turns out that in the land of overtraining, cyclists occupy a prominent spot. In fact, few other athletes seem capable of inducing such a bone-deep weariness. According to Dr. Snyder, this may be because of the concentrated way that cycling stresses the body. "Cyclists' muscles could become overtrained sooner because they're using mainly the quadriceps," she says. "Runners use more muscle mass. With cyclists, if the quads are tired, the rider will be tired."

It may come as a surprise that you needn't undergo a titanic training load to be overtrained. In fact, working folks who have sporadic and relatively light riding schedules may be the most likely of all to experience such problems, according to a study that reviewed overtraining.

"Less experienced athletes and those who train themselves may be particularly prone," according to his report. This is because these individuals either emulate the programs of elite riders or fail to recognize the symptoms of overtraining. In other words, it's all relative. Your 100-mile week of riding may be a post-race cooldown for a Tour de France pro, but if you rode only 20 miles in the previous week, your body could show all the symptoms of overtraining.

So how do you guard against the perils of overtraining? While most riders don't have access to the sophisticated measuring methods used by exercise physiologists, a few key indicators can be monitored.

Resting heart rate: Dr. Snyder's study showed a significant increase in sleeping heart rate, but it did not find much change in resting pulse first thing in the morning, the traditional measurement that most cycling coaches emphasize. Another study, in which runners doubled their training mileage, however, showed a morning increase of about 10 beats per minute.

Although these studies have different findings, they share an essential truth: Overtraining produces an elevated heart rate. Record your pulse upon waking under the same conditions each day, and beware of significant increases.

Disposition: While this may seem to be the vaguest possible index, it may be one of the most reliable. In one 10-year study involving swimmers, measurements of such things as anger, depression, and vigor were taken. As you might expect, these dispositions worsened markedly when training loads were doubled. When every pothole seems like a personal insult, beware.

Time trial performance: Dr. Snyder recommends doing a short time trial in similar conditions every other week while building up for a big event. "I wouldn't worry about a time that's 5 seconds slower," she says. "But if you're off by a minute, it could be due to overtraining."

Time trial heart rate: A drop of 10 beats per minute or so in your average heart rate can indicate overtraining. Some heart rate monitors can calculate average beats per minute. If yours doesn't, note the highest heart rate attained during the time trial. Should this begin declining, overtraining could be the reason.

The rebound effect: The key is whether your training regimen enables you to go faster, or longer, in your targeted events. If after a period of intense training you show no performance benefit, then you may not have rested enough. Moreover, if you continue to ride hard in the face of this evidence, you may end up overtrained.

"Overreaching could be part of your normal training cycle," says Dr. Snyder. "If you rest for a few days, you'll recover. But with overtraining it could require a month or two. The bottom line is that both will lead to detriments in performance unless you take days off."

Rest. It could be the most important training choice you'll ever make.

GLOSSARY

KEY CYCLING TERMS

aero bar: A handlebar that extends forward to allow a low, aerodynamic riding position with arms resting on padded supports. Aero extensions can be bolted to conventional drop handlebars.

aerobic: Exercise at an intensity that allows the body's need for oxygen to be continually met. This level of intensity can be sustained for long periods.

aerodynamic: A design of cycling equipment or a riding position that reduces wind resistance. "Aero" for short.

anaerobic: Exercise above the intensity at which the body's need for oxygen can be met. This intensity can be sustained only briefly.

apex: The sharpest part of a turn where the transition from entering to exiting takes place.

attack: An aggressive, high-speed jump away from other riders.

balaclava: A thin hood that covers the head and neck with an opening for the face. It's worn under the helmet to prevent heat loss in cold or wet conditions.

bead: In tires, the edge along each side's inner circumference that fits into the rim.

block: To legally impede the progress of opposing riders to allow teammates a better chance of success.

blood glucose: A sugar, glucose is the only fuel that can be used by the brain.

blow up: To suddenly be unable to continue at the required pace, due to overexertion.

bonk: A state of severe exhaustion caused mainly by the depletion of glycogen in the muscles because the rider has failed to eat or drink enough. Once it occurs, rest and high-carbohydrate foods are necessary for recovery.

boot: A small piece of material used inside a tire to cover a cut in the tread or sidewall. Without it, the tube will push through the tire and blow out.

bottom bracket: The part of the frame where the crankset is installed. Also, the axle, cups, and bearings of the crankset.

bpm: Abbreviation for beats per minute, in reference to heart rate.

break, breakaway: A rider or group of riders that has escaped the pack.

bridge, bridge a gap: To catch a rider or group of riders that has opened a lead.

bunch: The main cluster of riders in a race. Also called the group, pack, field, or peloton.

bunnyhop: A way to ride over obstacles such as rocks or logs in which both wheels leave the ground.

cadence: The number of times during 1 minute that a pedal stroke is completed. Also called pedal rpm.

carbohydrate: In the diet, it is broken down to glucose, the body's principal energy source, through digestion and metabolism. It is stored as glycogen in the liver and muscles. Carbs can be simple (sugars) or complex (bread, pasta, grains, fruits, vegetables). Complex carbohydrates contain additional nutrients. One gram of carbohydrate supplies 4 calories.

cardiovascular: Pertaining to the heart and blood vessels.

cassette: The set of gear cogs on the rear hub. Also called a cogset, cluster, or block.

categories: USA Cycling's division of racers based on ability and/or experience. "Cat" for short. In road racing, cat 1 through 5, with 5 being beginner. In mountain biking, pro, and cat 1 through 3, with 3 being beginner.

century: A 100-mile ride. A 62-mile ride is known as a metric century.

chainring: A sprocket on the crankset. There may be one, two, or three. Short version is "ring," as in "big ring" and "small ring."

chasers: Those who are trying to catch a group or a lead rider.

chondromalacia: A serious knee injury in which there is disintegration of cartilage surfaces due to improper tracking of the kneecap. Symptoms start with deep knee pain and a crunching sensation during bending.

circuit: A course that is ridden two or more times to complete the race.

circuit training: A weight-training technique in which you move rapidly from exercise to exercise without rest.

clean: In mountain biking, to ride through a difficult, technical section without putting a foot down.

cleat: A metal or plastic fitting on the sole of a cycling shoe that engages the pedal.

clincher: A conventional tire with a separate inner tube.

cog: A sprocket on the rear wheel's cassette.

contact patch: The portion of a tire in touch with the ground.

crankset/cranks: The part of a bicycle's drivetrain that transmits the rider's pedaling action into forward motion. A crankset consists of two cranks (or crank arms), one to three chainrings, and the chainring bolts that connect them together. Each crank arm connects a pedal to the bottom bracket. Crank arms are typically available in lengths from 165mm to 180mm to accommodate various sizes of riders.

criterium: A mass start race covering numerous laps of a course that is normally about 1 mile or less in length. "Crit" for short. Races typically last for a preset number of laps or a specific length of time, usually between 45 and 90 minutes.

cross-training: Combining sports for mental refreshment and physical conditioning, especially during cycling's off-season.

cyclocross: A fall or winter event contested mostly or entirely off pavement. Courses include obstacles, steps, and steep hills that force riders to dismount and run with their bikes.

disc brake: A braking system that uses a small caliper mounted near a front or rear dropout (usually on the left side) that clamps on to a stainless steel disc attached to the hub to generate a braking force. Disc brakes are the standard on modern mountain bikes and are becoming increasingly popular on road bikes. Their advantage is their superior brake modulation. They also work better than standard rim brakes in wet riding conditions.

domestique: A rider who sacrifices individual results to work for the team leaders.

downshift: To shift to a lower, easier-to-pedal gear—that is, shifting to a larger cog or a smaller chainring.

draft: To ride closely behind another rider to take advantage of the windbreak (slipstream), which requires about 30 percent less energy. Also called sitting in or wheelsucking.

drivetrain: The components directly involved with making the rear wheel turn. Composed of the chain, crankset, cassette or freewheel, and derailleurs.

dropout: A slot in the bike frame into which the rear wheel axle fits.

drops: The lower part of a downturned handlebar typically found on a road bike. The curved portions are called the hooks.

echelon: A form of paceline in which the riders angle off behind one another to get maximum draft in a crosswind.

electrolyte: Substance—such as sodium, potassium, or chloride—that is necessary for muscle contraction and maintenance of fluid levels.

epic: A remarkable bike ride due to its length, difficulty, elevation gain, and/or spectacular views.

ergometer: A stationary, bicycle-like device with adjustable pedal resistance used in physiological testing or indoor training.

fartlek: A Swedish word meaning "speed play," it is a training technique based on unstructured changes in pace and intensity. It can be used instead of timed or measured intervals.

fat: In the diet, the most concentrated source of food energy, supplying 9 calories per gram. Stored fat provides about half the energy required for low-intensity exercise.

feed zone: A designated area on a racecourse where riders can be handed food and drinks.

field sprint: The dash for the finish line by the main group of riders.

fixed gear: A direct-drive setup using one chainring and one rear cog, as on a track bike. When the rear wheel turns, so do the chain and crank; coasting isn't possible.

full tuck: An extremely crouched position used for maximum speed on descents.

gearing: The chain's position expressed as the number of teeth on the chainring and on the rear cog. The three most common chainring combinations are 53-39, 52-36, and 50-34. Cassettes typically come in 11-23, 11-25, and 11-28, though you'll also find some wider range 11-32 models. Also becoming more common are single chainring setups that are combined with 10-42 wide range cassettes.

general classification: The overall standings in a stage race. Often referred to as GC.

glutes: The gluteal muscles of the buttocks. They are key to pedaling power.

glycogen: A fuel derived as glucose (sugar) from carbohydrate and stored in the muscles and liver. It's the primary energy source for high-intensity cycling. Reserves are normally depleted after about $2\frac{1}{2}$ hours of riding.

glycogen window: The period within an hour after exercise when depleted muscles are most receptive to restoring their glycogen content. Eating foods or drinking fluids rich in carbohydrate enhances energy stores and recovery.

gorp: Good ol' raisins and peanuts, a high-energy mix for nibbling during rides. Can also include nuts, seeds, M&M's, or granola.

hammer: To ride strongly in big gears.

hamstrings: The muscles on the backs of the thighs; not well developed by cycling.

hang in: To barely maintain contact at the back of the pack.

headset: The parts at the top and bottom of the frame's head tube into which the handlebar stem and fork are fitted.

integrated seatmast: A feature of a frame that does not use a traditional seatpost. Instead, the seat tube is extended up past the top tube and is fitted with a cap that holds the saddle. Some integrated seatmasts must be cut to fit the rider's leg length, while others use capitals of different lengths to accommodate different leg lengths.

intervals: A structured method of training that alternates brief, hard efforts with short periods of easier riding for partial recovery.

jump: A quick, hard acceleration.

lactate threshold (LT): The exertion level beyond which the body can no longer produce energy aerobically, resulting in the buildup of lactic acid. This is marked by muscle fatigue, pain, and shallow, rapid breathing. Also called anaerobic threshold (AT).

lactic acid: A substance formed during anaerobic metabolism when there is incomplete breakdown of glucose. It rapidly produces muscle fatigue and pain. Also called lactate.

leadout: A race tactic in which a rider accelerates to his maximum speed for the benefit of a teammate in tow. The second rider then leaves the draft and sprints past at even greater speed near the finish line.

LSD: Long, steady distance, a training technique that requires a firm aerobic pace for at least 2 hours.

mass start: Events such as road races, cross-country races, and criteriums in which all contestants leave the starting line at the same time.

metric century: A 100-kilometer ride (62 miles).

minuteman: In a time trial (TT), the rider who is one place in front of you in the starting order. So called because, in most TTs, riders start at 1-minute intervals.

motorpace: To ride behind a motorcycle or other vehicle that breaks the wind. This is an advanced-level training technique used to increase leg speed and mimic actual race conditions.

mudguard: Fender.

nipple: A small metal piece that fits through a wheel rim and is threaded inside to receive the end of a spoke.

noodle: The L-shaped tubing piece found on the side of linear pull cantilever brakes.

off the back: Describes one or more riders who have failed to keep pace with the main group. Also referred to as OTB.

orthotic: Custom-made support worn in shoes to help neutralize biomechanical imbalances in the feet or legs.

overgear: Using a gear ratio too big for the terrain or level of fitness.

overtraining: Deep-seated fatigue, both physical and mental, caused by training at an intensity or volume too great for adaptation.

oxygen debt: The amount of oxygen that must be consumed to pay back the deficit incurred by anaerobic work.

paceline: A group formation in which each rider takes a turn breaking the wind at the front before pulling off, dropping to the rear position, and riding the others' draft until at the front once again.

pannier: A large bike bag used by touring cyclists or commuters. Panniers attach to racks that place them low on each side of the rear wheel, and sometimes the front wheel.

peak: A relatively short period during which maximum performance is achieved.

peloton: A French word meaning the main group of riders in a race.

periodization: The process of dividing training into specific phases by weeks or months.

pinch flat: An inner-tube puncture marked by two small holes caused by the tube being squeezed against the rim. It results from riding into an object too hard for the air pressure in the tube. Also called a snakebite.

power: The combination of speed and strength.

power meter: A cycling component training device that typically uses strain gauges embedded in the crank, hub, pedal, or crank arm spider of a bike to measure rider output in terms of watts.

preload: The adjustable spring tension in a suspension fork or rear shock. It determines how far the suspension compresses under body weight and how much travel remains to absorb impacts.

presta: The narrow, European-style valve found on most inner tubes. A small metal cap on its end must be unscrewed before air can enter or exit.

prime: A special award given to the leader on selected laps during a criterium or the first rider to reach a certain landmark in a road or cross-country race. It's used to heighten the action. Pronounced "preem."

protein: In the diet, a substance required for tissue growth and repair.

Composed of structural units called amino acids, protein is not a significant energy source unless not enough calories and carbohydrate are consumed. One gram of protein equals 4 calories.

psi: Abbreviation for pounds per square inch. The unit of measure for tire inflation and air pressure in some suspensions.

pull, pull through: To take a turn at the front of a pack of riders.

pull off: To move to the side after riding in the lead so that another rider can come to the front.

pusher: A rider who pedals in a large gear at a relatively slow cadence, relying on the gear size for speed.

quadriceps: The large muscles at the front of the thigh, the strength of which helps determine a cyclist's ability to pedal with power.

quick link: A special connecting link that allows derailleur-type chains to be disassembled and reassembled without the use of tools.

quick-release: A cam-lever mechanism used to rapidly tighten or loosen a wheel on a bike frame or a seatpost in a seat tube.

reach: The combined length of a bike's top tube and stem, which determines the rider's distance to the handlebar.

repetition: Each hard effort in an interval workout. Also, one complete movement in a weight-training exercise. "Rep" for short.

resistance trainer: A stationary training device into which the bike is clamped. Pedaling resistance increases with pedaling speed to simulate actual riding. Also known as an indoor, wind, or mag trainer (the last two names derived from the fan or magnet that creates resistance on the rear wheel).

road race: A mass-start race on pavement that goes from point to point, covers one large loop, or is held on a circuit longer than those used for criteriums.

road rash: Any skin abrasion resulting from a fall. Also called crash rash.

rollers: An indoor training device, similar to a treadmill for bikes, consisting of three or four long cylinders connected by belts. Both bike wheels roll on these cylinders so that balancing is much like actual riding.

saddle: The seat of a bicycle.

saddle sore: Skin problem in the crotch that develops from chafing caused by pedaling action. Sores can range from tender raw spots to boil-like lesions if infection occurs.

saddle time: Time spent cycling.

sag wagon: A motor vehicle that follows a group of riders, carrying equipment and lending assistance in the event of difficulty.

Schrader: An inner-tube valve identical to those found on car tires. A tiny plunger in the center of its opening must be depressed for air to enter or exit.

set: In intervals or weight training, a specific number of repetitions.

sit on a wheel: To ride in someone's draft.

slingshot: To ride up behind another rider with help from his draft, then use the momentum to sprint past.

slipstream: The pocket of calmer air behind a moving rider. Also called the draft.

snap: The ability to accelerate quickly.

soft pedal: To rotate the pedals without actually applying power.

speed: The ability to accelerate quickly and maintain a very fast cadence for brief periods.

speedwork: A general term for intervals and other high-velocity training, such as sprints, time trials, and motorpacing.

spin: To pedal at high cadence.

spinner: A rider who pedals in a moderate gear at a relatively fast cadence, relying on pedal rpm for speed.

spinning: A type of training involving stationary trainers and repeated intervals.

stage race: A multiday event consisting of various types of races. The winner is the rider with the lowest elapsed time for all races (stages).

stem: The component that attaches a bike's handlebars to the frame's steer tube. Choosing the correct stem length and angle are a key step in the bike fitting process.

straight block: A cassette with cogs that increase in size in one-tooth increments.

suppleness: A quality of highly conditioned leg muscles that allows a rider to pedal at high cadence with smoothness and power. Also known by the French term *souplesse*.

take a flyer: To suddenly sprint away from a group.

team time trial (TTT): A race against the clock with two or more riders working together.

tempo: Fast riding at a brisk cadence.

throw the bike: A racing technique in which a rider thrusts the bike ahead of his or her body at the finish line, gaining several inches in hopes of winning a close sprint.

time trial (TT): A race against the clock in which individual riders start at set intervals and cannot give or receive a draft.

tops: The part of a drop handlebar between the stem and the brake levers.

training effect: The result of exercise done with an intensity and duration sufficient to bring about positive physiological changes.

travel: In suspensions, the maximum distance a fork or rear shock can compress.

tubeless: A type of clincher tire in which the bead forms an airtight seal with the rim, eliminating the need for an inner tube. Allows bike tires to be run at extremely low pressures, for increased traction. Usually used in conjunction with a liquid tire sealant that helps prevent air from leaking in the event of a tire puncture.

tubular: A lightweight tire that is glued to the wheel rim and has its tube sewn inside the casing. Also called a sew-up.

turnaround: The point where the riders reverse direction on an out-and-back time trial course.

UCI: Union Cycliste Internationale, the world governing body of bicycle racing headquartered in Aigle, Switzerland.

upshift: To shift to a higher, harder-to-pedal gear; that is, shifting to a smaller cog or a larger chainring.

USA Cycling: The national governing body for cycling in the United States.

velodrome: A banked track for bicycle racing.

VO_2 max: The maximum amount of oxygen that can be consumed during all-out exertion. This is a key indicator of a person's potential in cycling and other aerobic sports. It's largely genetically determined but can be improved somewhat by training.

wheelsucker: Someone who drafts behind others but doesn't take a pull.

windchill: The effect of air moving across the skin, making the temperature seem colder than it actually is. A cyclist creates a windchill even on a calm day, a situation that must be considered when dressing for winter rides.

windup: Steady acceleration to an all-out effort.

ACKNOWLEDGMENTS

First and foremost, a heartfelt thanks to Ed Pavelka and his amazing team of contributors who collaborated on the first edition of the *Complete Book of Road Cycling Skills*. That list includes John Allen; Arnie Baker, MD; Edmund R. Burke, PhD; Geoff Drake; Jim Langley; Gary Legwold; Fred Matheny; Michael McGettigan; Rory O'Reilly; Jo Ostgarden; Robert M. Otto, PhD; Nelson Pena; Davis Phinney; and Julie Walsh, MS, RD. Together, this group of unrivaled experts laid the solid foundation of information, insight, and expertise that this latest edition was built around. Also thank you to the patient and knowledgeable expert sources who collectively aided in bringing this book up to date with the latest information, guidelines, and cycling techniques. That list includes Jeremy Powers; Scott Moninger; coach Frank Overton; Julie Emmerman, PsyD; Matt Pahnke, PhD; coach Mat Steinmetz; bike fitter Todd Carver; Scott Christopher; aerodynamic expert Chris Yu; Andrew Hammond; Derrick Lewis; and coach Trevor Connor. Finally, a tip of the hat to Mark Weinstein, Franny Vignola, and the rest of the incredibly patient and passionate Rodale Books team. And hugs and kisses to my wife, Lisa, and daughter, Cora, who continue to put up with my addiction to two-wheeled human transport in all its amazing forms.

ABOUT THE AUTHOR

An avid cyclist, Jason Sumner has been writing about two-wheeled pursuits of all kinds since 1999. He's covered the Tour de France, the Olympic Games, and dozens of other international cycling events. He also likes to throw himself into the fray, penning first-person accounts of cycling adventures from all over the globe. Sumner has also done extensive gear testing, written countless how-to articles, and is the author of *Bicycling 1,100 Best All-Time Tips* and the cycling guidebook *75 Classic Rides Colorado*. When not writing or riding, the native Coloradoan, who lives in the small mountain town of Crested Butte, can be found enjoying time with his wife, Lisa, and daughter, Cora.

INDEX

Boldface page references indicate photographs or illustrations. <u>Underscored</u> references indicate boxed text.

Fixed-gear bike, 30–31
Fluids. *See* Hydration; *specific type*
Focus
    association and, 151
    descending and, 41, 153
    on inspirational messages on bike
        frame, 145
    on oncoming cars, 52–53, 64
    performance and, 151
    positive thinking and, 149–50
    at training camp, 105
Food. *See also* Nutrition; *specific type*
    convenience-store, 132–34
    eating while cycling and, 130
    as fuel, 129
    hunger and, 129–30
    juicy, 137
    log, 113
    personal choices of, 131
    salty, 136
    selecting, 130
Fork of bike, checking, 76, **76**
Frame of bike
    material of, 5
    shape of, 172
    size of, 4–5, 7–8
Fruit, 133
Fruit-flavored yogurt, 132–33
Functional threshold power (FTP),
    118

G

Gatorade, 124
Gearing, 143. *See also* Gears
Gears
    aerodynamics and, 171
    cables, lubing or replacing, 78–79, **78**,
        81
    climbing and, 143
    descending and, 41
    downshift, 46
    gloves and shifting, 158
    in hill climb intervals, 103
    maximum heart rate and, 98–99
    pedaling and, 30–31
    progressive shifting, <u>174</u>
    for recovery ride, 178

for speed training, <u>174</u>
    standing and, 46
Gear. *See* Clothing; Equipment
Genital numbness, avoiding, 11, 13
Glasses for riding in rain, 162
Gloves, 13, 159
Glycogen, 88–89, 94, 129, 136
Glycogen depletion, 94, 136
Glycolysis, 88–89
Goals, cycling, x, 3, 149
Greek yogurt, 139
Group riding
    climbing and, 46
    "drop kicking" and, avoiding, 46
    finding groups and, tips for, 43–44
    handlebar position for, 14–15, **14**
    hand signals and, 45
    line and, holding, 45
    overlapping wheel of another rider
        and, avoiding, 46
    rhythm of, 46
    surging and, avoiding, 45
    technique, 44–46
Gym, training in, 156

H

Hammer technique, **16**
Hammond, Andrew, 17
Hamstrings, 11, 31–32, 109
Handlebar
    aero, 169
    climbing and, 13–14, **13**
    descending and, 15–16, **16**
    drops, 9, 15–16, **15**, **16**, 33, 37–38, 175
    on-bike position and, 9
    positions, 13–16, **13**, **14**, **15**, **16**
    tops, 8–9, 13–14, **13**, 144
    width, 9
Hands
    fatigue of, avoiding, 13
    holding handlebar and, 13–16, **13**, **14**,
        15, **16**
    on-bike position and, 8–9, 13
Hand signals, 45, 64
Head and on-bike position, 8
Headset of bike, 76, **76**
Health club, training in, 156